you got to **burn** to **shine**

john GIORNO

you got to burn to shine

HIGH RISK BOOKS

SERPENT'S TAIL

NEW YORK / LONDON

First published 1994 by
High Risk Books/Serpent's Tail
4 Blackstock Mews, London, England N4 2BT
and 401 West Broadway, New York, NY 10012

Library of Congress Cataloging-in-Publication Data

Giorno, John, 1936–
   You got to burn to shine : new and selected writings / John Giorno.
      p.   cm.
   ISBN 1-85242-321-8 (pbk.)
   1. Gay men—New York (N.Y.)—Literary collections.   I. Title.
   PS3557.I53Y68   1994   93-36151
   811'.54—dc20   CIP

British Library Cataloguing-in-Publication Data

   Giorno, John
   You Got to Burn to Shine: New and Selected Writings. — (High Risk)
   I. Title   II. Series

Book and cover design by Rex Ray
Typeset in 11/15 Janson and Futura Condensed Bold
      by Alabama Book Composition of Deatsville, Alabama
Printed in Hong Kong by Colorcraft, Ltd.

Contents

INTRODUCTION
"VOICES IN YOUR HEAD,"
by WILLIAM S. BURROUGHS

JOHN GIORNO BEGAN as an innovator of the school of Found Poetry. In his early work in the 1960s he used newspapers, advertisements and television to assemble a montage of word and image. This produced a déjà vu experience in the reader or listener, because he had seen or heard the source material in another context. He was the first poet to apply the revolutionary ideas of Pop Art to poetry, although many have imitated and developed upon his innovations.

When I first knew John in 1965, he was a very silent individual, hardly ever speaking. Then he underwent the testicular surgery commemorated in his poem *Cancer In My Left Ball*, and after that, for some reason, he became quite voluble. He also grew more and more serious about his Buddhist studies and practice, and at this time John is an accomplished practitioner of *wisdom-mind*.

The Romantic poet of the nineteenth century liked to think of his "ME," his very own personal thoughts and feelings, as something uniquely special and deeply mysterious. Many poets and prose writers still adhere to this viewpoint. But Buddhist meditation reveals the self-glorifying "ME" as trivial, illusory and very much the same from one person to another. Wouldn't we all like to be beautiful pop stars and billionaires? The dreary sameness of the mind laid bare. And the audience laughs with relief. Yes, we think just that way, all of us, so why pretend we don't?

The repetition that characterizes John Giorno's poetry is rooted in the basic nature of language, or symbolic representation, which is actually concerned not with communication, but with orientation in time: You wake up. You go to the bank. How many times will you repeat to yourself while you get ready to leave for the bank, "I have to go to the bank to go to the bank the bank the bank . . ." As if you could not get to the bank without repeating your intention to go there over and over to yourself.

And the audience recognizes this seemingly senseless repetition as part of their own mental processes— "Yes, our minds sound just like that." The changing emphasis on different syllables as the phrases are repeated helps to break apart the too-familiar "meaning" of the words, to crack them open and show their emptiness. This explicit realization conveys a feeling of liberation.

The function of art is to make us aware of what we know and don't know that we know. When Cezanne's paintings were first exhibited, some viewers were so incensed that they attacked the canvases with their umbrellas. You can't tell anyone anything he doesn't already know. They could not see that the paintings reflected still-life objects seen from a certain angle in a certain light. Others looked at Cezanne and said, "Yes, of course, I've seen a pear looking just like that." The experience of seeing, hearing, experiencing something that we already know, but do not quite know that we know, can be described as "surprised recognition."

John Giorno has brought forth a new form. It is not poetry in the classical line of Villon, Shakespeare, Wordsworth: "a powerful emotion recollected in tranquillity." (In tranquillity, and also in solitude. Poetry was a solitary act of evocation.) But John's poems are designed and created to be read aloud as part of a public performance. The emotion is immediate, a continuum that includes the future audience and the future performance. And John's live performances of his work are unforgettable; he writhes and sweats and shouts and whines, and you forget you are watching a man, losing yourself in his stream of words from the unconscious.

This has more in common with drama than with traditional poetry, but it is a drama without characters. Here, the *dramatis personae* are voices: to be heard, rather than read. And where do these voices come from? They involve a precognitive dialogue between John Giorno and his future audience:

Don't talk about it, it only makes it worse,
Today was one of the worst days of my life,
I hate every moment being here with you,
In the morning when I am shaving and I
cut myself
I know it is going to be a bad day a bad
day a bad day.

Sound familiar doesn't it?

I keep thinking about the same thing over
and over,
I keep repeating in my head what I said to
you,
the same sentence.

Tomorrow and tomorrow and tomorrow, round and
round, the dialogue taking off on its own, round and
round, day after day. Whom are you talking to, when
you talk to yourself? Is your self really your self? Isn't
there some other self in there with your self? John
Giorno raises these questions to an almost unbearable
pitch, to a scream of surprised recognition:

I'm a thief in an empty apartment
and I'm giving it all away,
I'm giving it all away!

The harshness and cruelty of some of the voices
speaking through the lines of John's poems point a
bright flashlight into your soul, as you recognize those
ugly thoughts. At the same time, the words are drained
of their "ugliness." This leads the hearer in the right

direction, toward nonattachment. As it says in the Tibetan Book of the Dead: if something is beautiful, do not cling to it; if something is repulsive, do not shrink from it. John's words help us to see that beauty and horror are only empty shadows playing on the mirror surface of original mind—which is featureless.

But John Giorno is also insidious. His litanies from the underworld of the mind reverberate in your head, and they get right into your nondominant brain hemisphere, your back-brain thoughts (you don't know too much about what's going on there), and ventriloquize your own thoughts.

One astronaut, when asked what he dreamed in space, said he didn't have any dreams at all, and certainly not in space, all indecent right in front of my astro-buddies. Anybody who doesn't have any dreams at all is precisely lacking in the attribute of vision: SEEING. And what we spend twenty-three billion oysters sending those clowns up to the moon for was they should SEE something, right? So now they won't take writers and artists into space as observers, who would be subject to see something? As the poet says:

> You reckon ill who leave me out—
> When me you fly, I *am* the wings!

Yes, maybe we will go along into space, invited or not:

> Heavily muscled Randy Scott,
> You're my favorite astronaut.
> Hunky Scotty, oh yooo-hooooooooooooo—
> I'm going to hitch a ride with youuuuuu!

One time, John Giorno and I considered forming a pop group called "The Mind Parasites." Because all poets worthy of the name are mind parasites, and their words ought to get into your head and live there, repeating and repeating and repeating. Try reading these poems aloud, let yourself go.

I remember the glory days of the "Red Night Tours" after the publication of my novel *Cities of the Red Night*, in 1981, when I went on the road with John from coast to coast, reading to college-age audiences in punk-rock music clubs and student union ballrooms. Then, as now, we were the closest friends, and we were a perfect team. John's rock-and-roll delivery never failed to electrify our crowds, and then I would go on stage with my carefully-chosen reading pieces, like a Grandpa from hell. I hope we changed a few minds along the way, infected them, perhaps . . . but now, it's *your* turn to get the bug.

STRETCHING IT WIDER

Some things
that work
in one
decade,
don't work
in the next,
so mark
it down
as a noble
idea
that failed.

And I did
what everybody

dreams
of doing,
I walked
away
from it
I walked away
from it
I walked away from it
I walked away from it,
and I never
went back,
without reconcile.

And since I
can't leave,
I love
getting drunk
with you
I love getting
drunk with you
I love getting drunk with you,
and give me some
more blow.

Nobody
ever gives
you what
you want
except by mistake,

and the only
things you
ever got
is what
you did for yourself,
cause you
hate them
and you're only
doing it
everyday
for the money,
you hate them
and you're only doing it
everyday for the money.

I know guys
who work
all their
life
and have got
a lot,
and something
happens to him,
and he loses
everything
just like that,
and I haven't
even got
that
and I haven't even got that.

Hard
work,
low
pay,
and embarrassing
conditions,
you are worse
than I remember,
and you're
home
and you're home
and you're home
and you're home
and you're home.

What is
a rat doing,
when it
isn't eating
garbage
or scaring you
on the street,
they're laying
around
like pussy cats,
you and I
sleeping in
the bed sheets,
warm
and cozy,

sliding
your legs
under the covers
and staying there.

You got to keep
down
cause they're shooting
low,
press your body
against the ground,
it's gravity,
the telephone
hasn't rung
once today.

If there is
one thing
you can not
and will not
do
is make
this world
a better
place,
if there's one thing
you can't do
is make the world
a better place,
if there's one thing

you're not going to do
is make the world a better place.

Cause you are
only successful
when you
rip
somebody off,
and everybody
I've ever known
who wants to
help somebody,
wants to
help themself,
and I'm a firm
believer in
giving somebody
enough rope
to hang themself.

You're standing here
watching all
these people,
and everything seems
a little
confused
and everything seems
a little confused,
I haven't got
anything to say.

The noose
is tightening
the noose is tightening
the noose is tightening,
and let me make
one more
further
observation,
when you
die,
you're going to die
with a hard-on.

If I didn't
have an
accident
I wouldn't
be here
If I didn't have
an accident
I wouldn't be here
If I didn't have an accident
I wouldn't be here.

Then there is
the reality
of the family,
your mother
and father,
them and

my mistakes
is why
I'm sitting
at a table
with a bunch
of stupid
jerks
on Thanksgiving
eating
a turkey
stuffed
with lasagna.

I'm spending
my whole
life
being with
people
I don't want
to be with
I spending my whole
life being with people
I don't want to be with
I spending my whole life
being with people
I don't want to be with,
and there ain't
no such thing
as family,
just people
you work with.

I love
completely
perverted
people,
you are my
best
sexual
fantasy,

I never got
that far with
scat
before
and I want to
remember it,
tireless
and I want to remember it,
tireless
and I want to remember it, tireless.

We make money
the old-fashioned
way,
we earn it,
the anchor
man
never leaves
the building,
and the only
difference

between me
and a preacher,
is he's
telling you
he has a way
out,
and I'm telling you
don't bother,
for you
there is
no way
out
for you there
is no way out
for you there is no
way out
for you there is no way out,
and it isn't
as though
you got anything
to lose.

Besides they
blocked
permanently
all
the exits
they blocked permanently
all the exits,
you and I
get to

stay here
forever
and it gets
worse
beyond your
imagination.

I would like
to give my
best
to all sentient
beings,
and before
I die,
I'd like
to de-tox
my mind
and tame
delusion,
but we are not
in a time
appropriate
to do this.

Tonight,
I want you
to give us
some drugs
and a little
alcohol,
if something

is good
people
like it
if something is good
people like it
if something is good people like it.

It looks
the way
it should
and you make me
feel good,
so let's
open it
up,
stretching it
wider
stretching
it wider
stretching it wider
stretching it wider
stretching it
wider,
and it shouldn't be
any trouble.

1982

BERLIN & CHERNOBYL

I was in Berlin
the week after
Chernobyl,
and we got caught
endlessly
in the warm
spring
rains,
big
fat
raindrops
filled with
radioactivity
splashing in
my face
and running down
my hair
and into my lips
over
and over
again,
big fat

raindrops
bejewelled
with radioactivity
soaked into
this black
leather
jacket
that I'm wearing
tonight,
great
wet
clusters
in the soft
black leather
shoulders,
100,000 ryms,
I only wear it
on special
occasions,
I feel like
Louis the 14th,
I got a coat
sewn with
10,000 diamonds,
and I got off
easy.

1986

LIFE IS A KILLER

Everyone says
what they do
is right,
and money is
a good
thing
it can be
wonderful.

Road
drinking,
driving
around
drinking
beer,

they need me
more than
I need them,
where are
you guys from,
stumbling off
into the night
thinking
about it.

When I was
15 years old,
I knew
everything
there was
to know,
and now that
I'm old,
it was true.

I got dragged
along on
this one
by my foot,
if I wasn't so
so tired
I would have
a good
time
if I wasn't so tired
I'd have a good time

if I wasn't so tired I'd have
a good time.

Tossing
and turning,
cause there's
a nest
of wasps
coursing
through your
bloodstream
cause there's a nest of wasps
coursing through your bloodstream.

If you think
about it
how could
it have come
to this
if you think about it
how could it have come to this,
it's coming
down the road,
right through
the red
lights,
and it's
there
and it's there
and it's there
and it's there.

Try your
best
and think
you're good,
that's what
I want
being inside you
that's what I want
being inside you
that's what I want being inside you,
endless
threshold,
and you hope
you're doing
it right.

How are you
feeling good
how are you
feeling
good
how are
you feeling good
how are you feeling
good
how are you feeling good,
you need
national
attention.

Cause essentially
all you
ever accomplished
was snort
some smack
and sit
on a zafu
watching
your breath.

How the hell
did I end
up
doing this
for a job?

I can't say
I don't need
anybody,
cause I need
the Buddhas,
and there's
nothing
I can say
about them.

Everyone is at
a complete
disadvantage,

you're being taken
to dinner
at La Cote Basque
and you're eating
9 Lives
liver
and drinking
wine,

the women
they are taking
prisoners,
I'm not going
nowhere,
I ripped up
my suitcases
I ripped up my suitcases.

Crank me
up
and keep me
open
crank me up
and keep me open,
crank me up and keep me open,
nothing
recedes
like success.

Whatever
happens
it will seem
the way
it seems
now,
and it doesn't matter
what you
feel,
how perfectly
correct
or amazing
the clarity,
everything
you think
is deluded
everything you think
is deluded
everything you think is deluded,
life
is a killer.

1982

HI RISQUE

I want
to scat
in your mouth,
I want you
to scat
in my mouth,
I want to scat
on your face
and rub it in

chocolate,
caviar,
and champagne,
absolute
preliminaries

pushing
the inner
envelope
to the limit,
one more
time,
mining
diamonds
with your tongue
for the crown
of one
of the kings
of hell,
when the going
gets rough
the tough
get gorgeous

squeezing
money
from the air
squeezing money
from the air,
snake
tongue,
stretching
your tongue
to the Buddhas,

diving
into the wreck
diving into
the wreck
diving into the wreck,
curiosity
and compassion,
and an exercise
in non-aversion,
fear
spiraling
from you
fear spiraling from you,
that gun's got
blood
in its hole

We do not do
this anymore,
but I still
think about it
when I'm
jerking off,
I was king
of promiscuity,
LSD,
crystal meth,
fist fucking
with 40 guys
for 14 hours,
it's worse

than I thought
and now,
every one
of them
I ever made
love to,
every single
one,
is dead,
and may they be
resting
in *great*
equanimity

We gave
a party
for the gods
and the gods
all came.

    1990

AIDS MONOLOGUE

I RUN THE AIDS TREATMENT PROJECT that helps people with AIDS by giving them cash grants for any reason: back rent, the telephone bill, medicine not covered by Medicaid, nursing, taxis, food. Money for anything that is needed. Money given with love and affection.

I began the AIDS Treatment Project in 1984, in response to the earth-shattering catastrophe of the AIDS epidemic. For me, it was an attempt, with a burning passion in my heart, to help individuals suffering from AIDS. The simple realization came to me that what a person with AIDS needs most is money.

A person with AIDS often feels abandoned and trapped in their daily circumstances; and a person with AIDS is often doing quite well, dealing with each problem as it arises, trying to build a stronger immune system, thriving and surviving as they say; and a person with

AIDS has often lost everything, and is about to lose their life. We try to relieve them, if only for a moment, from worrying about money. *We have never refused anyone money.*

My intention is *to treat a complete stranger as a lover or close friend;* in the same spirit as in the golden age of promiscuity, we made fabulous love with beautiful strangers, and celebrated life with glorious substances. "God, please fuck my mind for good!" Now that their life is ravaged with AIDS, we offer love from the same root, in the form of boundless compassion.

My way is to give money and strong emotional support. I do it personally and directly. I bring it to the hospital, or to the person's apartment, or he/she comes to my house, whatever is needed. Compassion without partiality, directed at every individual person with AIDS. I hug them as good friends, as they are, or as ten years ago I might have had fabulous sex with absolute abandon with the same stranger.

I am saying this because I want to encourage you to help someone with AIDS. I know you don't need to be convinced. You already know the facts, want to help, and do; but I'm saying it again, one more time, to inspire you to help someone or help someone you're helping some more.

Giorno Poetry Systems started the AIDS Treatment Project in 1984, and it has taken many shapes. We have given away over $450,000 individually and with much care. We run the Poets & Artists With AIDS Fund, the Tibetan Medicine AIDS Program, and we sponsor the annual Gregory Kolovakos Awards for AIDS Writing. In addition, we organize individual funds for anyone requesting it, providing a vehicle through which the person's friends can help. We also give support to small AIDS organizations.

Being generous doesn't cost anything. We give money free. It doesn't cost anything to give money. It doesn't cost anything for me to talk to you or for you to talk to me. You don't have to charge money for writing a check. You don't have to charge money for being professional. You just do it. Giving money is one of the sweetest songs anyone can sing.

I have never wanted to make the AIDS Treatment Project into another large AIDS organization with a big budget, staff and payroll. Giorno Poetry Systems receives no management fee or percentage. There are no salaries, no administration expenses, and no fund-raising fees. All work is given free and all money goes directly to help people with AIDS. Giorno Poetry Systems absorbs any miscellaneous expenses. I simply do what I do, whenever an idea arises to help a need, I follow it and make the idea come into being. Whenever I'm asked I can't say No. The point is: if I can do it, so can you.

I spend one or two hours a day, seven days a week, every week, every month, every year, and I am happy to be able to do it. I am HIV negative, through some miracle, as I am sure I came in contact with the AIDS virus but somehow I'm negative. I am a gay man; I am 55 years old; and I have lived most of my life being infinitely promiscuous, but for the mere last ten years.

I am saying this to encourage everyone who is HIV negative to help someone with AIDS, and help a stranger. It is easy to help a friend, or a relative, or a lover, because you are attached to them, and you want to, but help a stranger with the same feeling as you would a friend. This might seem like a job for medical professionals or for HIV positive people to help themselves from self-interest. It is our job, too. It won't kill you and you don't get infected or tainted. In fact, it is a purifying experience.

When you become familiar with a problem, fear falls away, allowing help to arise from simple compassion. The intention is indiscriminate compassion, non-discriminating compassion, not making distinctions between people, not, I'll help this one but not that one 'cause I don't know him, but helping everyone with AIDS. There is always just enough resources to help everyone. Give whatever you can, and loving kindness.

Attending the dying is giving quality time (as they say in the trade). Digging in and (getting your hands dirty) being careful and mindful, and bringing your natural generosity to all people with AIDS. I believe the moment of death is the most important time in a person's life. We try, in our small way, to (help) empower him/her for his passage through that time. I radiate from my heart to his heart, trying to give him/her peace, warmth, spaciousness, blissfulness, and strength. I sit with him in the moments after death, resting in *great equanimity*.

1992

SCUM & SLIME

Optimism,
trust,
fearless
authority,
and disaster

eating filth
and transforming it,
with white
intentions
into black
compassion.

I want to be
filthy
and anonymous

I want to be filthy
and anonymous
I want to be filthy and anonymous.

Open your
eye lids
and see it
looks good,
drinking
poison
and in each sip
on your lips
is wisdom
mind.

I like warm air
going over
my skin,
billions
of world
systems,
and your body is
crawling
and crashing
into the surf.

Pouring
money
down
another
hole

pouring money
down another hole
pouring money down
another hole,
and keep it
hidden.

When Adam
and Eve
were in the Garden of Eden,
God asked Eve
not to do
two things,
not to eat
the fruit
and not to go
swimming,
so she ate
and went for a swim,
and that's why
the ocean smells
of fish.

You and I are
sleeping on
a cement
and linoleum
kitchen floor,
you look like
a television
sitting on
a refrigerator.

I would crawl
through a mile of shit
to suck off
the last guy
who fucked her.

We don't take
drugs
no more,
we sit around
praying
for money,
don't do anything
drastic,
when you are with
a lover
you have no
control
when you are with a lover
you have no control
when you are with a lover you have
no control.

I want to be
filthy
and anonymous,
scum
and slime.

What's going on
in here,
it looks like
everyone is
underwater,
give me
a break,
I'm dead
and I'm asleep
I'm dead and I'm asleep.

1985

SUCKING MUD

5000
years ago
there was this
hero
and heroine,
where's the heroin,
and they were
at war
for a thousand years,
when one would
succeed
the other would
fail,
one day

she got really
angry
and they had
a duel
to the death,
they flew up
into the sky
and had a star wars
confrontation,
he took
his sword
and threw it,
and stuck it
into her heart,

she was so angry,
just as she
was about
to die,
she released
her period,
and where
the drops
of blood
fell
to earth,
tobacco
plants
grew,
and that's the origin
of cigarettes.

Do anything
you want
but don't come
in my mouth
do anything you want
but don't come in my mouth,
suck
those sweet
pits,

That's the way
I like them,
drunk
and all dressed up,
eating it
live
in one gulp,
sucking
mud
sucking mud
sucking mud
sucking mud
sucking mud,

fist
and forearm,
push it,
stick it,
punch it,
break it open,

smash it,
suck it,
make it feel good.

You got
to keep
a light
hand,
if you want
to touch
their heart,
you got to keep
a light hand,
if you want to touch
their heart,
your body feels so
good,
completely
attached to
embracing
warmth.

Bring me
your dead,
even though
I don't know
what to do,
bring me
your dying
and let me
know them,

and don't trip
over the confetti,
the winds
between
the worlds
cutting like
a knife.

1986

NONE OF THEM WANTED TO GO

I'VE SEEN THE BEST MINDS of my generation die horrible deaths from AIDS.

Rudy Wurlitzer called me early on the morning of March 18, 1989, with the news that Robert Mapplethorpe had just died in a Boston hospital. "Robert had a *grand mal* at the moment of death," said Rudy. "It was heavy!" The next day I spoke to Lynn Davis, Rudy's wife, who had been with Robert in his room in the hospital when he died.

The last four days of Robert Mapplethorpe's life went like this: Robert refused to die, he refused to give up. He had been sick with AIDS for years, and his body was disintegrating from various AIDS diseases. His mind and mental faculties remained sharp and clear. Robert had heard that Dr. Jerome Groupman in Boston had a radical new therapy for AIDS. Robert rented a deluxe rock 'n' roll tour bus, the quintessence of luxury, normally used by Mick Jagger on tour, and made the trip. When he arrived at Boston's Deaconess Hospital, he was too sick to undergo the treatment and too weak to return to New York. Robert held court, surrounded by his retinue, being imperious and endearing. One of Robert's last boyfriends went up to Boston to visit, of whom William Burroughs said, "He has a sincere but untrustworthy face."

Robert died four days later in a *grand mal* or severe epileptic seizure at the moment of death, screaming and shaking violently, vomiting blood; he was crazed and demented, blood spewing from his mouth, blood trickling and farting from his asshole, blood splattered all over the hospital room. He was absolutely refusing to die, with an almost demonic attachment, refusing to leave this life. A male hospital nurse said, "I have never seen anyone die like that."

After Robert's death, as his body lay on the hospital bed, Lynn said, "Robert looked very peaceful, like an angel!" Lynn loved Robert. I hope he was, but the body often looks peaceful because it has stopped functioning and is inert. Indeed, the family and friends often think the dead person has gone on to heaven or a better place because they love the person, but actually the consciousness and soul of the dead person is screaming, *"I'm dead and I don't want to be dead!"*

Robert Mapplethorpe had a great love of beauty and was very attached to life, as witnessed by his great photographs that fix impermanence, his vast collections, and his fame. To die in a *grand mal* is not the best way to die. The state of a person's mind in the moments before death carries over with the consciousness after death. The spasms and confusion could influence the moments after death, which is one of the most important times in a person's life: when there is a chance for liberation into the vast, empty expanse of original nature. Having an epileptic fit at this time might block the consciousness and leave the person angry he's dead. I don't know what happened after Robert Mapplethorpe died, but there is the possibility that the absolute worst happened.

Among the many possibilities: the person who refuses to believe he is dead stays in this world. Traditionally this kind of being is called a spirit or ghost. The problem is that a spirit experiences great suffering because it can see everything (the dead can still see, hear and feel through habit, only having lost their body, similar to seeing when asleep and dreaming), but is separated from what is perceived as belonging to it. The dead can influence events, depending on how powerful the person was in life, and events can be affected in a positive or negative way. The fame, of both Robert Mapplethorpe and Andy Warhol, greatly increased after their deaths, and I venture to say that they both possibly, for a while, serviced their careers from the dead.

That night after Robert Mapplethorpe died, I was in my loft on the third floor at 222 Bowery, and I went to get myself another drink. I had first met Robert in 1976, and again with Patti Smith, and my designer, George Delmerico, had gone to Pratt with Robert in 1971–75, and Robert did the brillant photographs for the LP cover of my album *Sugar, Alcohol, & Meat*. It was about 7 P.M. and I had one light vodka and soda, and smoked a joint. I was drinking from an art deco Lalique glass, from a set of Lalique crystal I had inherited from an aunt, and each glass was worth $400. I use those glasses on special occasions honoring demons and gods. I was wondering where Robert's consciousness was, and what state he was in. When I lightly put the glass with half-melted ice cubes down on the table, the glass broke. A ring of glass separated one-half inch down from the top, as if a psychic buzzsaw of his consiousness from hell had swooped down and cut it off. I heard and felt the noise. I was shocked. A four-inch wide perfect ring of Lalique, thin and fragile. What an amazing sign! I thought, Thank you for nothing, Robert (who had such a great love for beautiful objects)! And I let the matter rest, feeling sad for him.

WE ALL HAVE to die sometime and there are better ways to do it. Terry Clifford's death was one of the best. Terry, 39, died on August 10, 1987, apparently not of AIDS but of diseases similar to AIDS. Healthy and beautiful, Terry fell sick and was dead in three months from lymphoma, lung and breast cancer, and meningitis causing lesions on the brain. In the hospital, Terry asked two of her doctors for an AIDS test, and they threw back their heads and laughed, saying, *"What do you want an AIDS test for? You have lymphoma. Do you want more bad news?"* We learned afterwards that the doctors believed that Terry did not have AIDS.

Terry Clifford was a great meditator in the Tibetan

Nyingmapa Buddhist tradition. She had been on strict retreats for more than five years. She had received many of the highest teachings from the highest lamas. Her teachers were H. H. Dudjom Rinpoche and H. H. Dilgo Khentyse Rinpoche. She had great realization and skills in the highest Tantric yogas. She prepared for death—the moment when the consciousness leaves the body—with the transcendence and humility of a saint, and with the discipline and courage of an Olympic athlete who trains for one moment in competition. Terry died perfectly and attained Enlightenment.

A week before Terry died, we were sitting in her living room, laughing and telling each other profound gossip, and having a good time. Terry was talking with clarity and brillance, then she paused and said, *"John, excuse me for a moment."* She closed her eyes and turned aside. This was when the cancerous tumors in her brain were growing voraciously. Terry rested in meditation, seeing the hallucinations as delusion, realizing their empty nature, and recognizing in whatever arises the simultaneity of the arising and dissolution in the great expanse. She took no pain killers and felt no pain, in the sense that you don't really feel pain in a dream if you realize it's a dream. After a few minutes she turned to me, smiling radiantly, and said, *"You have no idea what goes on inside my head!"*

When her death suddenly came, she handled it with perfection. She understood impermanence and had fully realized absolute wisdom and emptiness. She asked two friends to help her sit up in a chair in her bedroom and dissolved her consciousness into *great equanimity*, resting in the great bliss and clarity of Primordial Wisdom Mind.

Terry died with great peace, beyond hope, and had no panic, no fear, no lingering, and she was gone. There was no cold wind. Everything was warm, happy, and radiant. Her bedroom filled with dazzling brightness. She demonstrated nonattachment, accepting what is, not fighting it and not clinging to it. She was surrounded by her Dharma friends, never lost interest in them, and had great compassion for all around her. She was a Buddha manifesting Enlightenment and going to a Pure Field. I don't know what happened after Terry Clifford died, but there is the possibility that the best happened.

1991

(LAST NIGHT) I GAMBLED WITH MY ANGER AND LOST

You're laying down
watching TV,
monitoring
the telephone
automatic
answering
machine
when
it rings,
and I don't want to
talk to you
cause I know
what you want,
it's a great

step forward
when you listen
to your friends
call and
dissolve them
one by
one.

I prefer
wandering alone
in the bardo,
sexual
warmth,
being one
pointed,
bacon fat
and blood,
and it doesn't matter
if you like
being here
or whether it's
good for you,
you must
stay here
you must stay
here
you must stay here
you must stay here
you must stay here.

This is a time
to lay low,
no heroic
endeavors
or noble
efforts,
but that is
not to say
we can't make
a deal,
and I want to
punch him
in the face

I want to put
my fist
in his face again,
one more
time,
cause at some
point
you gotta be
pragmatic,
and I don't want
anybody
telling me
about solutions
and I don't want anybody
telling me about
solutions
and I don't want anybody telling

me about solutions
and I don't want anybody telling me
about solutions,
they don't work.

You are on hold,
and you're trying
to give this
a wash
and a rinse,
crate it
and ship it,
and when I got
nothing else
to think about,
I like to
think about
the things you
did wrong,
what you did
wrong,
and how I'm
telling it to you
and getting
rid of you,
and I always
got to have
someone
like that
to think about
and I always got

to have someone like
that to think about
and I always got to have
someone like that
to think about
and I always got to have someone
like that to think about
and I always got to have someone like
that to think about.

I am up there
past my
elbow
going to
my shoulder,
big
and leave
it in,
and I think you
can handle it,
teach me
some manners,
tell me
how to be
polite,
make me
want to
smear it
in your face,
make me want
to smear it in

your face
make me want to
smear it in your face,
in your mouth,
and your nose,
and your holes,
drastic
and desperate,
and it shouldn't be
fatal.

I like video
like that,
that makes you
feel good,
deep
intimacy,
long
tenderness,
bankrupting
yourself
with generosity
bankrupting yourself
with generosity
bankrupting yourself with generosity.

I'm waiting
in line
with my groceries
in the supermarket,
and I want to

get away
without
incident
and I want to get
away without
incident
and I want to get away
without incident.

I like drinking
vodka
by myself,
at home
alone
smoking
dope,
nothing is
more exhilarating
nothing is more exhilarating

It is so
hopeless,
you can't begin
to imagine,
so you want to
go soft,
you want to go
gentle,
cause when you go
easy,
you get your

hand in,
Boeing F-18
Fighter-Bombers
flying in
formation,
homing in
beyond
digital,
fire
the absolute
guns,
fire the
absolute
guns
fire
the absolute guns
fire the absolute guns
fire the absolute guns,
last night,
I gambled with
my anger
and lost.

1983

EXILED IN DOMESTIC LIFE

I'm standing
in the hall,
I pushed
the button,
and I'm waiting
for the elevator,
you are alone
and you are unstable
and you're not sure
it's OK
anymore,
exiled
in domestic
life

exiled in
domestic life
exiled in domestic life.

Nobody does
it for you,
you got to
do it
all by yourself,
and I've been
brutalized
and I've been brutalized
and I've been brutalized
and I've been brutalized.

I would rather
be dead,
than 18 years old,
and a poet,
and if I can
do that,
I can sit
on somebody's
face
I can sit on
somebody's face
I can sit on somebody's face,
and feed.

I want to
sleep

hugging
someone
over and
over again
I want to sleep hugging
someone over and over
again,
and cuddling
in the morning,
cause it's
healing
my body
in my heart,
it's safe
to be married
these days
it's safe to be married
these days.

When you got
lots of negative
thoughts,
they are big,
and powerful
and wonderful
they are big, and powerful
and wonderful
they are big,
and powerful and wonderful,
it's their
job
to get it up,

it's not
your problem.

If it isn't
black,
it's not
good,
and it's not going
to work,
you don't feel
a razor
blade
you don't feel a razor blade,
and I like juice,
your skin
smells like
an old sponge
soaked in
alcohol,
and this place
stinks.

A hundred
million
years ago,
the geophysical
adjustments
that made petroleum
from primordial
forests,

maybe 100 million
years from now,
will transform
the plastic
in our garbage
into something
better than
diamonds.

The reason
it's good,
is cause
I work
all the time,
and I've been spending
the rest
of my time,
laying on
the bed
with my girlfriend
watching TV,
and I want her
to tell me
wisdom
when she doesn't
know she is
and I want her to tell
me wisdom
when she doesnt't know
she is
and I want her to tell me

wisdom when
she doesn't know she is.

What are you
slapping your
hands
together for,
do you want
me to slap
your face?

1983

GREAT
ANONYMOUS SEX

Keith Haring and the Prince Street Toilet

ON SUNDAY NIGHT, January 27th, 1985, I gave a dinner for eight in my third-floor loft at 222 Bowery. William Burroughs was staying in the Bunker. The famous young artist Keith Haring was invited to meet William and me. James Grauerholz arranged the dinner, and said, "The concept is famous gay men around William." The guests were: Keith Haring, David Del Tredici, Ira Silverberg, Paul Alberts, and Juan Dubose, Keith's boyfriend. The dinner was awkward. Keith's enthusiasm was a pleasure.

I served crabmeat mousse, lobster fra diabolo, chocolate truffle pie, and endless joints and booze. Keith and Juan had been up all the night before, Saturday night, dancing at the Paradise Garage. Juan was crashing, and spent the evening in the hall, sitting on the steps, sleeping with his head in his hands. I invited Laurie Anderson because she had never spent any time with William, other than at photo shoots or in separate dressing rooms backstage on the tour in 1981 when I released the LP album of the three of us called *You're The Guy I Want To Share My Money With*. Laurie arrived over two hours late, when we were finishing eating, and was the only woman. For me, the best thing about the dinner was that it ended.

Keith invited William, James, and me to visit his studio the next day. William didn't feel up to it (we all had disastrous hangovers). At 1 P.M., James and I went to Keith's studio at 611 Broadway. Keith had just arrived and was beginning his day, and his helpers and assistants—beautiful young boys—started appearing. It was wonderful seeing his brilliant work. James and I stayed for about forty-five minutes. It was a joy being with him.

Keith said, "I have a present for you!" and he gave me a painting on paper, a red and black gouache, of a man with a big dick at the end of which was a hand holding a baby. Keith's joyous celebration of life.

"Thank you!" I said. "Are you sure? Such a magnificent gift and I scarcely know you. Thank you!"

"I owe it to you," Keith said. "When I came to New York in 1978, one of the first things I did was go to the Nova Convention. William and Brion and you completely changed my life. I want to thank you."

"Keith, it's not necessary!" I said, wide-eyed and overjoyed at the startling beauty of my new acquisition.

The year before in Paris, I had visited Brion Gysin,

who said Keith Haring had come to see him. I said that I hadn't met Keith, but I loved his work. Brion looked quite surprised, and said, "You should know him! He knows you! He's a great fan of yours!"

Keith seemed a little familiar (I had been introduced to him at a crowded party and forgot), but he seemed familiar in another way, then it hit me. I once had great anonymous sex in the Prince Street subway toilet with a young guy I didn't know, but who, I remembered, had recognized me. I remembered his face, it was Keith. We had intense sex, almost a love affair, for over an hour, a long time for subway sex on the run.

In July 1982, at about 11:30 in the morning, I was taking the subway uptown. I had an appointment with my printer. I went into the Prince Street station, and immediately into the men's toilet, as I always did. Rather then just stand around a boring platform waiting for the train, I'd go in the toilet, and all I had to do was take out my cock, wave it around, and some guy would go down sucking. It was much more fun than waiting on the platform, and a great pleasure. When the train came, whether I came or not, I'd put my dick back in my pants, run out and jump on.

That morning I was getting my cock sucked when a young good-looking but slightly homely kid with wire-rimmed eyeglasses, who was standing next to me, put his arm around me, and we started kissing. His eyeglasses were getting crunched on his face and he took them off. He was a plain boy with pale white skin, but with a very attractive quality. We were hugging and sticking our tongues in each other's mouths, while the other guy was sucking on my cock. After a while, I noticed an unusual passion in the kid. He was making love with great energy and focus, affection and delight, different than the routine going on around me. The guy's heart was pouring love and I went with the flow. I sucked the kid's cock (it was cut, not that large but very hard). He sucked my cock, with his eyes looking up into mine. Two guys with poppers kept sticking them in our nostrils for us to take big sniffs. We continued alternating sucking each other's cocks. He managed a couple of times to get my cock all the way down his throat and I fucked his face, moments of surrender for both of us. The onlookers jerked off watching us.

I began to realize that the kid recognized me as the poet John Giorno. This always was disappointing for me because the spontaneously arising play where there was no past, present, or future, only freshly appearing moments seemed compromised by dumb concepts. I looked at him and wondered how much he knew, and whether he was a poet or an artist. My guess was that he was an art student, and that he went to the School of Visual Arts. None of this mattered because the kid seemed very pure, and we were making love.

The toilet stank of cigarette smoke, disinfectant, and piss, which in the hot humid morning bit the nostrils, almost making me gag. The clarity was sharpened by the underlying constant danger that a cop or plainclothes policeman could at any moment walk in the door and arrest everyone. When someone entered the toilet, everything stopped, and he had to be checked out, whether he was straight or gay, trouble or OK. It took about a minute for my intuition to say Yes or No. I was lucky and never got busted. I was also always in a state of constant desire, of wanting something, no matter what I was getting, I wanted more. Never at ease, never completely relaxed, and always looking over my shoulder. The danger heightened the pleasures.

A couple of times I went back to making it with one or another of the guys I had been doing it with before I met him, but the kid kept standing close, and sort of psychically pushing them away and pulling me to him. Another time I turned back and he was smoking a joint. He and I smoked together, occasionally passing it to one of the others. There were about ten guys, some sad and ugly, some old men, but a few really good-looking men. One was being rimmed and he came spraying ropey cum on the filthy concrete floor.

We kissed, holding each close as hard as we could. We pressed our bodies together strongly, trying to push inside each other, so there would be one body, one dick, one heart. I wondered whether he was thinking of the Burroughs concept of the union of two minds, *The Third Mind*, or the Tibetan view of being dissolved in one taste.

It was a ninety-degree steamy July morning and the air was soaked with humidity. The toilet crowded with men made it perhaps over one hundred degrees. The kid and I were completely hyperventilated, and our body temperatures burned, and we poured sweat, which is always an exhilarating high. You got to burn to shine. We got to burn some more. Burning away all concepts, releasing bliss trapped in our hearts.

Every once in a while we would relax and take a breather, for about sixty seconds, before we lunged at each other again. He was wearing a white T-shirt, washed-out blue jeans with holes at the knees, and sneakers. An art student, I thought again, as I saw some splashes of paint on his pants leg. Or an artist, but how can he afford the exorbitant rent of a Soho loft, or maybe he works for a famous artist (I hope not), or maybe he really goes to the School of Visual Arts and is going to see a gallery show.

During all these discursive thoughts, another discursive thought kept repeating itself, *"And he recognizes me, and he knows who I am, and he recognizes me, I wonder how much he knows?"* The great thing about anonymous sex is you don't bring your private life or personal world. No politics or inhibiting concepts, no closed rules or fixed responses. The great thing about anonymous sex is spontaneity. The kid recognized John Giorno and was possibly bringing the nonexistent famous poet and the baggage of that expectation to cloud our anonymous sex of great bliss.

Five guys circled us with dicks in their hands, jerking off. Somebody stuck a popper in my nostril and his, and we fell into each other's mouths and bodies again. Everyone vanished but the two of us. In the ecstasy of sheer stoned delight, we were in a dream of formless divine presence. We were both gods playing in a god world, demons playing in hell, and spirits loving spirits, with the feeling of how completely empty and boring sex is, and how completely blissful at the same time. The grass and poppers, besides their chemical properties, numb the nerve ends, and allow the natural clarity of the Mind to flow free.

Someone straight came into the toilet who didn't look cool. We took a break. I asked him, "What's your name?" Not that I wanted to know, but simply to extend with generosity the openness we felt for each other. At that very moment a train roared into the station. The kid said his name in the deafening noise, "Keith!" Vaguely hearing and not quite caring, I said, "What is your name?" The kid said slightly indignantly over the roar of the train, "Keith!" I was a bit surprised that he should have the slightest presumption that I would know his name. We were anonymous. The straight man left and somebody stuck a popper in my nose and we started again. Men with dicks sticking out of their pants stood around watching us.

I unbuckled the kid's belt and he pulled down his pants. I turned him gently around, slowly eased in the wet head and slipped my cock into his ass, and he pushed to me and took it all. His ass was slightly lubricated with vaseline. I wondered if it was from this morning or last night, and if he had someone's cum in his ass. That thought made me hotter and the grease made my dick feel even better. Someone started rimming me, had his face buried in my ass, his tongue in my asshole, and was nibbling and sucking. This is also a great pleasure for me. I fucked the kid, gently at first, then gradually as hard as I could. Sweat poured off us in sheets. From the depth of the inebriating darkness of that underground cave, stretching my cock to the sky, I shot a big long load of cum, straight and glorious. Perfectly arisen and accomplished, and perfectly dissolved back into primordially pure empty space.

After I came I rested in his arms for a while. The kid pressed his dick against me, and obviously wanted to come, too. I sucked his cock and I wished he'd come so I could stop doing it. I got up and kissed him, and tried to jerk him off, but he gently pressed my shoulder for me to go down. He wanted to come in my mouth. Now, giving blow jobs is not my specialty, and since I'd just come, I couldn't have felt less like doing it, but this kid was special, and I wanted to give him back something he really wanted. Gagging, I kept at it. The kid arched his back and started writhing, thrusting his hips forward and sinking his shaft all the way down my throat. He came in flood of thick gooey cum. It oozed from my lips as I swallowed. I got up and he kissed me, tasting his own cum in my mouth. In 1982, I knew very well about AIDS, but I thought this kid has such pure intentions, how could he have AIDS?

I said goodbye and I was out the door in a flash, onto the train going uptown. It always was a shock entering the straight world of a car full of grim people sitting dumbly with suffering on their faces and in their bodies, and their minds in their prisons. I had an appointment with my printer to see the color proofs of the album cover of my new LP called *Life Is A Killer.*

In July 1982, 24-year-old Keith Haring had just

joined the Tony Shafrazi Gallery and was about to have his first one-man show in October 1982, which turned a young, relatively unknown artist (he had been doing the subway drawings on the black panels for a year) into a world-famous superstar. In January 1985, when Keith came to dinner in my house, his body had changed slightly, becoming more solid from self-empowerment, and gaining an aura from power.

The Prince Street subway toilet happened in 1982 and we know from the record that Keith Haring suspected he was HIV positive in 1981, when he discovered early symptoms of AIDS, such as swollen lymph glands and thrush. When I gave Keith the blow job, he was HIV positive. Keith died of AIDS on February 16, 1990. Even though I swallowed his cum, somehow now in 1993 I am HIV negative and in excellent health, one of many miracles.

I have always remembered that anonymous kid for opening himself so extraordinarily, for allowing a great moment of fabulous transcendent sex, motivated by genuine love, trying to radiate enough compassion to fill the world. This kid opened himself up more than someone does in a subway toilet, opened himself up more than someone generally does with a lover, wife or husband. Of the countless great sexual encounters in the golden age of promiscuity, I have always remembered two as symbolizing all the others: the kid in the Prince Street toilet and the black man at the Everard Baths. I thought of us as the combat troops of love liberating the world.

All New York subway toilets were closed in the late 1980s, to discourage promiscuity and prevent the spread of AIDS. All the great public toilets of the world, the *pissoirs* of Paris, scenes of fabulous sex for centuries, are all now closed. Their demise seems like a dream come true for puritanical forces, a great victory for conservatives, the Fundamentalists won the lottery. The loss of ecstasy in unlikely ordinary places seems a great loss for everyone, particularly young people beginning their sexual activity. I regret that young people don't have the good fortune and opportunity we had.

Keith and I became good friends. Anything I asked him to do, he did tirelessly, with great devotion. Keith did the art for the cover of my LP album called *A Diamond Hidden in the Mouth of a Corpse*, illustrated my poem *Sucking Mud*, emceed my AIDS benefits, came whenever I invited him, and after his death, the Art Outreach Fund for Aids, which he established with George Mulder from the sale of the silk-screen print *Silence = Death*, gave $48,000 to my *AIDS Treatment Project*, among many other things.

Keith and I never talked about the Prince Street subway toilet. I never tried to have sex with him again (although I would have liked to) because I knew his obsession was with Black and Hispanic boys. Maybe he would have liked to, too, but neither of us made a move. Keith said in John Gruen's biography of him that his obsession with boys was maybe an excuse for him not committing to more fulfilling relationships. Keith also said, *"I firmly believe that sexual relationships—a deep sexual relationship—is a way of truly experiencing another person—and really* becoming *that other person."* And I agree with him.

1993

I DON'T NEED IT
I DON'T WANT IT
AND YOU CHEATED ME OUT OF IT

I'm old
and I'm bitter
and I'm going
to tell you
what
I think,
money
and politics
spoiled it
completely
money and politics

spoiled it completely,
and then
I learned
to like it,

and you're trying
to get
through
the rest
of the day
and you're trying
to get through
the rest of it
day
by day,
and at the very
best
you can only
keep it
hot
for 3
months,

I'm lazy
and I don't
want
to do
nothing,
except
what I
have to do,

tight
as a crab's
ass,

now I
want you
to stay
down
below
the waist
and under
no circumstances
come
above
the shoulders,
and I want you
to sniff
around
and keep
sniffing
keep sniffing,
you want to
walk away
with the smell,

you're off
on your own
and you're running,
I'm not
going out
tonight,

cause it's
more
trouble
than it's worth,
you're going
to stay
here
and drink
you're going to stay
here and drink
you're going to stay here and drink,
sitting in
the brown
velvet
chair
having a good
time
by yourself,

I'll tell
you something,
you think
you're so
great,
well
everybody
thinks
you're a joke,
it's a miracle
I've survived,

what
kind
of an artist
are you
anyway,
you do
nothing
but lay
around
in bed
all day
watching
TV,

I don't
need it,
I don't
want it,
and you cheated
me out
of it
I don't need it,
I don't want it,
and you cheated me
out of it
I don't need it,
I don't want it,
and you cheated me out of it,

take it
to the limit

one
more
time,
you gotta
make 'em
come
you gotta make
'em come
you gotta make 'em
come
you gotta make 'em come,
and then
fake it
for yourself,
I want you
to give
it to me
I want you to give it to me,
cause I
need it,
making
money
and having a good
time,

sheer
pain
and I love it,
take it
where you
find it
and give it

everything
you can,
tenderness,
intimacy,
and I'm glad
this one's
over,

thank you
for telling
me what
I did
was successful,
I love
being serviced
I love being serviced,

you're only
trying to
make them
fall in
love
with you
you're only trying
to make them fall
in love with you,
and then
rip
them off
as nicely
as you can,

and you keep
working it
over
again
and you keep working it over again,
trying
to score,

I spent
the whole
week
having meetings,
telling
people
how
well
we're doing
and how
great
everything is,
I'm going
to make it
this time,
baby
I want to
make it
perfect,
and you
give
and you give
and you give

and you give
and you give
and you give
and you give
and you give,
you give some
more,
and keep on
giving
again,
and give
until
it hurts,
only you're
high,

and you don't feel
it hurt,
it don't hurt
bad,
and you forget
it hurts,
and give until
it really
hurts
and give until it really hurts,
then I'm
not going
to give you
one
more
God damn

thing
ever
in any
lifetime,
you get
nothing
you get nothing,
nothing,

I'm waiting
for tomorrow
so I can
go to
work

I'm waiting for tomorrow
so I can go to work,
I got
an appointment
at 11
and I like
working
more
than being
with anyone,
and I'm laying
on the bed sheet
waiting
for enough
time to
pass
for me

to go to
sleep
for 5
minutes,
cause I
got to
get up
early,

thinking
it over
again
thinking about it
over again,
I'm re-running
a film
clip
of what
I was saying
this morning
on the telephone,

I got the
I don't
want to
do it
anymore
I got the I don't
want to do
it anymore,
I don't want

to do anymore
fund-raising,
and as a matter
of fact
I refuse
to raise
10 cents
for anyone,
I don't believe
the lie
anymore,
she had to
back off
cause she
was singed,
if I'm going
to hustle
I want to
hustle
for myself,

and in answer
to your question,
you should
think of me
as being
dead,
you know
after
a few
months

it's hard
to remember
somebody,
and after
a year
it's trying
to remember
a party
I went to
last year,
I thought
you'd learn
to love me
but I guess
you never
will
and I thought
I'd learn
to love you
cause you
feel so
good,
but it was
pizza,
quiche,
or beef
Wellington
take
out,
you missed
giving me

what
I want
you missed giving me
what I want,

I don't
care
for my life
or anyone
else's,
I'm an old
man,
and in 5
or 6 years
I'll be
falling
apart,
so I want
$100
pledges,
and I want
them as
fast as
they can
come,
poetry,
politics,
pragmatism,
and friends,
I never
thought

it would
end up
just
turning
a buck,

all I
want is
publicity,
cause
at least
it gives
a false
feeling
of being loved,
and sells
books,
everything
you thought
you understood
is a mis-understanding
or completely
wrong,
paralysis,
fear,
and deceit,

I don't
recommend
to anyone
to be alive,

and I can't imagine
anyone
wanting to
be alive,
except if
they're completely
deluded,
and I don't recommend
being born
again
anytime
anywhere
ever,
you're only
asking
for trouble
you're only asking for trouble,

you're floating
at the high
water
mark
and you already
spent
your whole
life
trying
to stay
afloat,
concentration,
will-power,

and endurance,
I'm trying
to get
through it
just like you,

nobody
told me
what to do,
so I took
what I
wanted,
you just
skidded
out of
control
you just skidded
out of control
you just skidded out of control,
the worst is
at this moment
happening,
you hit
a bank
of snow,

I'm a tough
old
fag
and I know
what I'm

talking
about,
we've got
a completely
different
situation,
"John,
it's time
for defense,"

I like
the feel
of a gun
in my hand
I like the feel
of a gun in my hand,
Smith
and Wesson
44 Magnum
Model 29,
3 tons
behind
that bullet,
my hand wants
to be holding it
my hand wants to be holding it,
picking up
responses,
safety
and power,
the world

outside
is a threat
and we're building
ourselves
a jungle
fort,
surface
to air
missiles
surface to air missiles,
increase
deployment,
readiness
alert,

cause tonight
the air
is jagged
with some
more slightly
dangerous
aspects,
I can't
see it
but I can
feel
the threat,
so I want
double

protection
I want double protection,

I love
the feeling
of being armed
with weapons
and I love the feeling
of being surrounded
by well-armed
attendants,
summon
the Secretary
of War,
thank you
for doing
what we
want you
to do,
I got
a will
of iron
and strength
of steel,

we're living
on a rough
street,
increase
expenditures
for defense,

surface
to surface
missiles,

reduce
debt,
pay your
American
Express Card
bill,
be gracious,
humble,
and seemingly
accessible
to everyone,
you're a movie
star
beyond
your wildest
imagination,

comrades,
long
has it been
since we've
drawn
our swords
shining,
you want
it
you got

it
you want it
you got it
you want it
you got it
you want it
you got it
you want it
you got it
you want it
you got it
you want it
you got it
you want it, you
98 got it
you want it, you got it,

an extreme
sadness
if you let
yourself
think,
glorious
weapons
systems
disguised
in ordinary
life,
heroin
and the samadhi
of the gods,

I'm completely
alone
and I love it
I'm completely alone and I love it,
can't you
tell it's
the best
thing
about
yourself,

tell me
what you
do with
trash,
tell me how
you treat
trash,
tell me what
you do
to it,
you flush
it down
the toilet,
there's
nothing
I love
about you
but I love
the way
you love me,

I'm having
myself
a little
love
and tenderness,
cause it's
all I
ever wanted
in the first
place,
warmth
and intimacy,
world
class
cup
cuddling
on LSD,
you know
how to
give me
exactly
what I
need,
we're doing
a double
backstroke
in an Esther Williams
movie,
making
money

and having a good
time
making money
and having a good time
making money and having a good time,

you always
get everything
you want
only you
get it
after you
stop
wanting it,

I'm not
going to
think about
anything
and I don't want
to work
anything
out,
if you only
knew
how sweet
and powerful
it is
to have no
expectations,

and be ruthless
and hungry,

and regarding
the possibility
to stop,
regarding the possibility to stop,
the decision
has been received
from the Cabinet,
delivered
by the Secretary
of State,

abort
mission
to final
Enlightenment,
take yourself
to the nearest
Buddhafield
if you learned
how,
and if you
didn't,
you got
a whole
lot
coming,

so I'm going
to make it
easy
on you,
kid,
your BMW
broke
down
on the freeway,
and you're walking
into the blackness
with this guy
holding
a flashlight,
and you come
out
with a funny
taste
in your mouth,
and keep
smiling.

1981

COMPLETELY ATTACHED
TO DELUSION

I'm going
to live
forever
and I want
to fly
I'm going to live forever
and I want to fly,

take me
to wardrobe,
you got a hangover
and you're crashing,
coming
down,

get it
up,
pull
on it
for awhile,
full
dress
is with
a smile,
warmth
and cheer,
I like
cocaine
sprinkled
on my pussy,
Air Force One
is waiting
on the runway,
keep
the dice
on the table,
you're coming
in on
a roll
you're coming in on a roll,
keep it
coming,

I love
being
with you

cause
we're on
drugs,
when
you got
it bad
we got
it good,
is it
big
enough
for you,

I want
to spend
the rest
of my life
in a Holiday
Inn
I want to spend
the rest of my life
in a Holiday Inn
I want to spend the rest
of my life in a Holiday Inn,

there are
no surprises,
breakfast
in bed
between
the cool

bed sheets
sliding
your legs,
just
work
and sex
and drugs
in New York,
and when
I come
down
all I
want to be
is high
again,

rather
than hang
around
here
feeling
tired,
everybody
I know
is a junky
everybody I know
is a junky
everybody I know is a junky,

we just
drank

ourselves
some beer,
and I want
to sing
my songs
over
and over
again,
all
I've ever
known
is dissatisfaction,
change,
and I want you,

you got that
slightly
paranoid
sinking
feeling
you got that slightly paranoid
sinking feeling,
like when
you got
hepatitis
everything
looks
yellow,
this is
where

I started
out

you think
you woke
up from
sleeping
and you feel
you're dreaming,
the telephone
is ringing,
and you're afraid
he doesn't
like you
and you're afraid
he doesn't like you,
but then
he would
have said
I'll see you
Saturday,

I don't
want to be
left alone,
I didn't
mean
to mislead you,
I just
wish you

were somebody
I loved,

I'm asleep
and I'm dreaming
and I'm remembering
this time
I'm dreaming,
you're sitting
having a cheeseburger
you're sitting having a cheeseburger
at the counter
with the napkin
dispenser,
salt
and pepper
shakers,
on 7th
Avenue,
Mama,
I always
love
losers,

you've done
the best
you can
and it wasn't
altogether
that good
you've done the best

you can
and it wasn't altogether
that good,
I put
muscle
in it
for as long
as I could,
and given
all you
wretched
people,
my bad
karma,
and Murphy's
Law
that if the worst
can happen,
it will,
and it was
a complete
failure
and it was a complete failure
and it was a complete failure

I'm tired
of people
grabbing
at me,
and I don't
want

anybody
cause you
don't get
nobody,

you boxed
yourself
into another
corner
you boxed yourself
into another corner,
you can't
go
ahead
and you can't go
back,
you just
got to go
out,
and I know
how to
go out
cause I
gone out
before,
recurring
patterns,

I just
watched
these two

guys
rob
an automobile
with a wire
hanger,
they rummaged
through
the back
of this station wagon,
said Nada
Nada and
walked
away,
then a few
minutes
later
this German
Shepherd
came by
and took
a leak
on the car
just missing
the window,

I'm having
myself
a little
love
and affection
I'm having myself a little

love and affection,
and the right
combination
of drugs,
I'm thinking
I want to
thank you,
and keep
on doing it
cause you're
doing it
right,
keep on doing it
cause you're doing it right,

loving you
all
over again,
while it
seems
monumentally
sad,
and I don't
trust
anybody
and I don't trust anybody
and I don't trust anybody,

standing
straight
on the bed,

right-wing
sex,
we're doing
water
sports,
I'm giving
it to you
in a slow
stream,
the way
you like it,
I love
to feel
your throat
swallowing,
this Bud's
for you
the king
of beer
is coming
through,

and it looks
like it
should be
feeling
good
and it looks like
it should be feeling good,
but I
don't

feel
nothing,
you're the
only one
getting it
cause you
want it
so much.

and a black
guy
once
said to me,
he said
a black man
once
told him,
"anytime
anybody
tells you
to look
up
at the sky,
you know
they got
their hands
in your pockets,"

you're keeping
me from
what

I want
to be doing
you're keeping me
from what I want to be doing
you're keeping me from what
I want to be doing,
from becoming
Enlightened,

I'm a thief
in an empty
apartment
and I'm giving
it all
away,

you learned
about
impermanence,
I love
impermanence
cause I know
everything
is going
to change
and I'm going
to leave
here,

I wish
you'd come

so it'd
end
I wish you'd come
so it would end
I wish you would come
so it would end,

I got
the feeling
I did
something
wrong,
you de-railed,
I don't have
anything
to sell
and I don't want
to buy
anything,
I don't have any
ideas,
I don't
know
and I don't
care
to know,

my meditation
is a complete
failure
my meditation is

a complete failure
my meditation is a complete failure,

one
more
time,
I can't wait
to get
back
to New York,
MDA
and I want
to marry you,
get a
meal
in a minute,
I want
my money
now,

you can
eat
crackers
in my bed
anytime,
you can
kick off
the covers
and open
up
the windows

wide,
your mommy's
rich
and your daddy's
good-looking,

I just
did myself
some heroin,
this is
the way
I've been
waiting to
feel

this is the way
I've been waiting
to feel
this is the way I've been
waiting to feel,

you were
told
about
patience,
now
you
understand,
nothing
ever
changes
nothing

ever changes
nothing ever changes,
seems you
would
have known
you'd fall
from nowhere
into nothing.

1980

ANDY WARHOL'S MOVIE
SLEEP

WHERE WERE YOU in '63, when JFK was shot?

I was with Andy Warhol.

I was a poet working for a brief time as a stockbroker on Wall Street. The news that JFK was shot in the head came over the Dow Jones at 1 P.M. The Board room was dumbstruck. The first thing I did was call Andy Warhol. I had spoken to Andy several times that morning, and just twenty minutes before. I asked him if he'd heard. "Yes," Andy said, someone had just called him. I ran out of Fahnestock & Co. and took a taxi to Andy's house on Lexington and 87th. We sat on the Tiffany couch amongst the clutter, watching the live TV coverage from Dallas. We heard Walter

Cronkite say, "President Kennedy died at 2 P.M. on November 22nd, 1963." We started hugging each other, pressing our bodies together and trembling. I started crying and Andy started crying. We wept big fat tears. It was a symbol of the catastrophe of our own lives. We kissed and Andy sucked my tongue. It was the first time we kissed. It had the sweet taste of kissing death. It was all exhilarating, like when you get kicked in the head and see stars.

I didn't particularly like Kennedy and I had never voted. Even though he was charming and sympathetic, to become president he had to have made all the bad deals and compromises, and be the most corrupt among the worst of them. We all knew how corrupt his father, Joseph Kennedy, was, bootlegging and passively supporting Hitler, and it was his father's money that had bought the White House. JFK and Jackie were glamorous, a definite plus, but he was just another dumb, ambitious politician, even though his heart presumably was in the right place. He had the vitality of youth, after all the old men presidents who came before him. Everything seemed possible; but I never thought about it when he was alive.

His assassination changed everything. He became an instant deity. "They shot my man!" I said exuberantly. "His death is the best thing he ever did!" Jackie was live with JFK's blood on her skirt. I had a rush of bliss watching the live TV coverage and hearing them talk about the blood and brains on Jackie's skirt, and how she refused to change her clothes. She was a world-class act. It was the first blood sacrifice of the decade.

I heard it as the death knell of the 1960s. There was so much unexpressed optimism, the moment of JFK's death seemed the absolute indication of the complete failure of everyone's aspirations, portending what was to come. The omen.

Andy and I went into the front room. Everything brilliantly radiated disaster. *"I don't know what it means!"* Andy kept saying in his inimitable voice. We tried to think about continuing the day. The telephone rang and Andy answered it. I went home and that night we met at 8 o'clock and went to a party. The first person we met was Bea Fitler. It was an electrifying night in New York.

Two days later in the afternoon on the Sunday after Thanksgiving, Andy and I went to a party at Billy Kluver's in New Jersey. Billy was a laser engineer at Bell labs, who also worked with artists and technology. Wynn Chamberlain drove us in his car. Andy and me, Marisol, Bob Morris, and Jill Johnston. We were on a winding suburban road in the freezing cold, getting near to Billy's. I had a small transistor radio pressed to my ear. This was almost two decades before the Sony Walkman and lightweight earphones were invented. I was trying to listen to the Ronettes and the Shirelles, "It's my party and I'll cry if I want to," when through the static noise came the news bulletin from Dallas that Oswald had been shot. "Somebody's been shot," I said, but everyone in the car kept talking. "Somebody else has been shot in Dallas." Nobody listened to me. They were talking art world gossip. "Andy, someone else has been shot, besides JFK, just now in Dallas." At that moment with the radio pressed to my ear, I heard a replay of the shot that killed Oswald minutes before. "I just heard the shot!" Andy was the only one listening to me.

When we arrived at the party, Billy greeted us at the door, and said "Oswald, the guy who killed Kennedy, just got killed by someone called Ruby!"

"*Oh, I don't know what it means!*" said Andy. We were all laughing. It was stunning.

There were about thirty of us in a ranch house, most of the Pop Artists (this was before they became famous): Patty and Claes Oldenburg, Jim Rosenquist, Bob Indiana, George Segal, Yvonnne Rainer, among others; Bob Rauschenberg and Steve Paxton had just left. Olga, Billy's wife, gave me a Bloody Mary. Everyone was drinking Bloody Marys. Andy had a can of Coke. Everyone was wide-eyed and exhilarated. I had a slight attack of paranoia and I said to Andy, "I don't know why I'm here!"

"*I don't know why I'm here!*" said Andy.

Everyone was laughing scattered about the house. We spent the afternoon taking turns in the living room watching the live TV coverage from Washington of the casket with JFK's body being moved from the White House to the Capitol. Jackie Kennedy wearing the black suit with the black veil over her face, walking in the freezing cold at the head of the cortege, leading the Heads of State and dignitaries, Charles de Gaulle taller than anyone, Emperor Haile Selassie, Queen

Fredrika of Greece. It was so electrifying. Andy kept saying *"I don't know what it means!"* The image of Jackie walking with the black veil seemed so incredible and so strong, it was burned in our hearts, later giving rise to Andy's paintings of Jackie with the black veil. "She's so fabulous!" said Andy. "It's the best thing she's ever done!"

The next morning I got to Andy's house at 11 o'clock for the JFK funeral. We sat on the couch in front of the TV, in the back room on the first floor, watching the whole thing for hour after endless hour, the casket being carried from the Capitol to the Cathedral to Arlington Cemetery. By then it was deadening and the first media OD, for me and for everyone, the first ever. Andy answered the telephone every once and awhile, and a few people came by and visited briefly (Robert Frazer and Irving Blum, separately, among others). Every so often Andy went downstairs to see his mother, who was watching on her TV in the kitchen where she slept. Andy said she was very upset.

After they lit the eternal flame in Arlington, I went home and spent the rest of the afternoon in bed. I met Andy at 8 o'clock that night and we went to a party. I liked being with Andy, more than being at the parties.

THE YEAR BEFORE all this happened, in 1962, I saw Andy at various parties. I was at the first show of Pop Art at the Sidney Janis Gallery on October 31, 1962, the Halloween that forever changed the art world, when Rothko, Motherwell, and other establishment heavies resigned in protest and outrage from the Sidney Janis Gallery. Three days later I was at the opening of Andy Warhol's first show at the Stable Gallery, with the breathtaking *Gold Marilyn Monroe*, *Campbell Soup Can*, *Coca Cola Bottles*, and other gorgeous paintings. Andy's show opened on November 3, 1962, the day of JFK's Bay of Pigs, and on everybody's mind was the possibility of nuclear war and complete disaster. All of it set the exhilarating mood for Andy's opening. Something new was in the air and Eleanor Ward's Stable Gallery was an electromagnetic field. Everyone knew it was the first great art show about something completely different. Wynn Chamberlain asked Andy, "What do you think?"

"I don't know what it means!" said Andy, standing in the crowd. I hadn't met Andy yet. Wynn introduced me as a young poet. I shook Andy's limp-wristed hand and looked in his eyes, and he said *"Ohhh!"*

On April 28, 1963, Wynn Chamberlain invited Andy, me, and a friend of his named Bobo Keely, to dinner in his loft on the top floor at 222 Bowery. This was the first time I got to know Andy. Spring comes suddenly in New York, the weather had just turned warm that day and it was chilly that night, but spring fever was in the air. Wynn cooked a gourmet dinner. We were going to the Judson Dance Theatre to see Yvonne Rainer's new piece, *Terrain*.

At dinner we talked about Bob Indiana's new show at the Stable and the current gossip. Andy mentioned he had a problem because he had to do a piece for the 1964 New York World's Fair and he didn't have an idea. Henry Geldzahler had selected twelve Pop artists to do works. Andy was asked to do something for the

New York State Pavilion, a ten-sided building designed by Philip Johnson, and he had to do ten huge pictures for the top of each side. *"Oh, I don't know what to do!"* said Andy.

We were eating coq-au-vin and drinking white wine. Wynn said "Andy, I have a great idea for you. The Ten Most Wanted Men! You know, the mug shots the police issue of the ten most wanted men."

"Oh, what a great idea!" said Andy.

"My boyfriend is a cop," said Wynn. "He can get you all the mug shots you want. He brings a briefcase of them home every night . . . But I'm thinking of the Ten Most Wanted Men sheets they put in the post office every month."

"Oh, what a great idea!" said Andy. "But Robert Moses has to approve it or something . . . I don't care, I'm going to do it!"

Wynn Chamberlain had a lover, Jimmy O'Neill, who was gay and a New York City policeman, half Italian and half Irish, and he was gorgeous. Jimmy was a third-generation cop. His grandfather was a captain and his father was a captain. Jimmy was hip. He gave Andy a big manila envelope filled with crime photos, mug shots, archival photographs, and the Ten Most Wanted Men.

Andy made ten enormous silkscreen paintings, each twenty-five square feet, for the New York State Pavilion. Of course when they were hung and Robert Moses saw the *Ten Most Wanted Men*, he freaked out and rejected them. Andy painted silver over them, mirroring the silver period at the Factory, getting him through the crisis, and more publicity.

There were hundreds of police photos in the envelope from Jimmy O'Neill. These photos also gave rise to some of the Disaster paintings.

IN THE SPRING of 1963, Andy and I started seeing a lot of each other. Every morning there was a plan for that night. Once or twice a week we went to see underground movies. This was the very beginning of the phenomenon called the *underground movie*. We'd go to the Bleecker Street Cinema or the Gramercy Arts Theatre or wherever they were playing. There was Jack Smith's *Flaming Creatures* (which we saw an endless number of times), Ron Rice's *Chumlum*, Taylor Mead's *The Queen of Sheba Meets the Atom Man*, and Kenneth Anger's *Scorpio Rising*, among others. They were great, but most of the other movies were horrible.

"They're so terrible," said Andy sitting in the blackness between reels at the Bleecker Street Cinema. *"Why doesn't somebody make a beautiful movie! There are so many beautiful things!"*

A week later Andy bought his first Bolex 16mm camera. He didn't know how to use it. He would ask a lot of dumb questions to filmmakers or whoever he happened to be with, like "How do you focus it?"

A week after that Andy and I went to Old Lyme, Connecticut, to visit Wynn Chamberlain for the weekend. Marisol and Bob Indiana also came. They were also visiting Eleanor Ward, owner of the Stable Gallery, who rented the stone icehouse converted into a small cottage next to Wynn's farmhouse. We went up by train the Saturday of Memorial Day weekend 1963. The weather had just turned incredibly hot.

That night Wynn gave a dinner party. We were all up till four in the morning. It was a sweltering ninety-degree night. I got really drunk off of 140-proof black rum. Andy didn't drink, he did speed, Obetrol. I passed out when my head hit the pillow. I woke up to take a piss as the sun was coming up. I looked over and there was Andy in the bed next to me, his head propped up on his arm, wide-eyed from speed, looking at me. "What are you doing?" I said bleary with a rubber tongue.

"Watching you!" said Andy.

I woke again and Andy was still looking at me with these Bette Davis eyes. "What are you doing?"

"Watching you sleep!"

I went back to sleep, and woke every once and awhile to see if he was still doing it. I woke again to take a piss and Andy was sitting in a chair at the front of the bed in the morning light. The next time I woke up, he was laying with his cheek on the pillow drowsily looking at me. It was 11:30 in the morning, boiling hot, my body was streaming with sweat, and did I have a hangover. "Why are you looking at me?"

"Wouldn't you like to know!" Andy laughed cynically.

When I woke up the next time, Andy was gone. It was 1:30 in the afternoon and he had watched me sleep for eight hours. From this was born the idea for Andy Warhol's movie *Sleep.*

On the crowded New Haven railroad back to New

York, Andy said, "I want to make a movie. Do you want to be the star?"

"Absolutely!" I said getting closer to him in the jam-packed sweating train. "What do I have to do . . . I'll do anything!"

"I want to make a movie of you sleeping!"

"I want to be a movie star!" I said enthusiastically. *"I want to be like Marilyn Monroe!"* This was before the word "Superstar" was invented. And before Andy expropriated the word "Superstar" from Jack Smith. The air-conditioning on the train was broken and it was hot. "That's what I've been asking you for!"

The week before, sitting on the Tiffany couch with the rolls of paintings in the back room of his Lexington Avenue house, Andy said, *"I should give you a present . . . I mean I want to give you a gift . . . What can I give you?"*

"I want to be like Marilyn Monroe!" I said intensely, drunk and stoned.

Andy just laughed, *"Oh John!"*

ONE NIGHT IN June 1963, after a party, Andy and I took a taxi uptown. We stopped by my place, a small carriage house at 255 East 74th Street. Andy came up to check out the bed for shooting *Sleep*, available light, electrical outlets, where he would set up his tripod, etc. I was sitting in a 17th-century Spanish chair when all of a sudden Andy was on the floor with his hands on my feet. One thing led to another and he was kissing and licking my shoes. I had always heard he was a foot fetishist, all those years designing shoe ads for Henri Bendel and Bonwit Teller.

There was Andy Warhol on his hands and knees, licking my shoes with his little red tongue. Too good to be believed! I thought, with a rush, "He's sucking my shoes!" It was hot. My shoes were covered with saliva. I got some poppers to make it better. Then he took my shoes off and started licking my feet and shrimping my toes, which I love. It was a great moment. Andy had a fragile and delicate approach to sex. I jerked off while Andy kissed my legs and sniffed my crotch. Then Andy licked the big gobs of white cum from my hand and stomach. Andy had a hard-on in his black jeans. I wanted to finish him off, but he said, "I'll take care of it."

I never wanted to make it with Andy. He was physically unattractive. But I loved him and he was the most fascinating person in the world in every way. He happened to be ugly, he understood that, and no one wants to be compromised. Andy was a voyeur anyway. He wanted to see it, he didn't want to touch it. He wanted to look. Occasionally, I let him suck my cock, out of compassion for his suffering. I was fascinated that he wanted to do my shoes. When you're young, you can always get it up.

The art world was homophobic, and an ever-present threat. Anyone who was gay was at a disadvantage. An artist overtly with a boyfriend was at a complete disadvantage, and could ruin his career. De Kooning, Pollock, Motherwell, and the male power structure were mean straight pricks. No matter their liberal views, they deep down hated fags. Their disdain dismissed a gay person's art. On top of it, those guys really hated Pop Art. I was a poet and I didn't want anything from them, and they didn't know I was alive (their wives and girlfriends really liked me), but they weren't cruel to me. I am a witness to their being cruel to Andy Warhol. Andy got around homophobia by making the movie *Sleep* into an abstract painting: the body of a man as a field of light and shadow.

ONE NIGHT IN early July 1963, Andy and I were going to a party. Andy asked me to pick him up at the Firehouse, his new studio on 87th Street between Lexington and Third Avenue. He had just rented it and started working there. It was a former NYC firehouse and it looked like an abandoned garage. There was an enormous cement ground floor and an enormous cement second floor. Andy had Jerry Malanga clean only the floors, the walls were filthy. "Andy, it's so chic!" I said, as he gave the tour.

"Oh, I know my dear, it is so chic!" said Andy, very pleased with himself.

Andy Warhol was painting the silver *Elvis* pictures. We went upstairs and there on the floor were eight life-size Elvis Presleys with gun in holster, silkscreened on one huge piece of canvas. Andy had painted the silver background the day before and had silk-screened the black Elvis image that day. They were magnificent, glittering like diamonds on the bleak cement floor. I was shocked, seeing something great and entirely new for the first time, beyond comprehension. I gasped, and pranced around in front of them, making exclamations of joy. "They're a breakthrough!"

"*I know, they're so beautiful!*" said Andy, really happy. For me, it was blissful. The newest moment of spontaneous accomplishment. He'd done it again. Sex and death. The silver '*Elvis*' paintings lay there radiating power. The deity perfectly arisen and the deity who made them arise.

"*They need a lot of work done . . . on them,*" said Andy.

We talked for a little while, then we were late for the party. We got ready to leave amid another burst of enthusiasm about the *Elvises*. Andy put out all the lights, except for the staircase light. We started walking toward the stairs, talking and leaning against each other. It was another hot sweaty night. As we reached the top of the stairs, we started hugging each other, and hugging each other more, and I stuck my leg between Andy's legs, and lifted him up a little.

I lost my balance and we fell backwards down the stairs, down the steel-lipped cement steps. Head over heels, we landed with a crash, Andy on top of me, and rolled over and over, down the industrial steps. Wrapped in each other's arms, down and down. My first thought was that the worst had happened. Then I tried to protect Andy. I absorbed my blow as I hit each step, then simultaneously I pulled him on top of me to absorb his blow, and in between I knew the antidote to catastrophe was to relax and roll, like a rag doll. The firehouse first floor ceiling was twenty-five feet high, with one long flight of stairs coming down. Hugging each other, we kept bouncing down from step to step. It was totally wonderful. Mayan gods, head over heels being thrown off the pyramid to the lower realms, we were descending gods. I wasn't getting hurt and I was trying my hardest to keep Andy from getting hurt. We landed at the bottom in a pile. There was nothing but very bright white light. No time and no space. One of those rare moments when in a state of shock caused by great physical trauma, one's mind shuts down for an instant, and one gets a glimpse of another pure realm. What a shock! After the moment of white light, there was another long blissful moment. In god world time, it might have been 100,000 years. Then we stood up, started laughing, and both said simultaneously *"What happened!"*

"Are you OK?" I managed to say.

"I don't know . . . Let me think," said Andy sweetly.

"Hold on to me," I said trying to stabilize the catastrophe. Somehow I knew neither of us had gotten hurt. "Are you OK? . . . Did you get hurt?" I started feeling him for broken bones.

"I'm OK . . . Are you hurt?" said Andy.

"I never get hurt." Then after some stupefied moments, there was nothing to do, but laugh uproariously. "You didn't break any bones?"

"I don't think so," said Andy. *"Did you?"*

"I have thick bones. They never break." We were hugging each other and laughing. "I feel totally great . . . Are you all right?"

"I think so."

"Are you sure?"

"I don't know . . . You could have killed me," said Andy.

"Andy, don't be silly. I kept getting under you to take each of your falls." When you're young, your body often never gets damaged.

"You tried to kill me!" said Andy.

"Don't be silly!"

"You're dangerous to be with!"

After a while we calmed down, got our equilibrium, and went to the party. The first thing Andy said on arriving at the party was, *"John tried to kill me. He pushed me down the stairs!"*

My feelings were very hurt. "Andy, how can you say such a thing! . . . It was the most important moment in your life!"

The single huge canvas of *Elvis Presleys* was rolled and sent to Los Angeles for Andy Warhol's first one-man show at the Ferris Gallery in September 1963. Irving Blum cut the canvas into eight pieces that became the eight famous silver *Elvis* paintings.

In 1977, Glenn O'Brien interviewing Andy for *High Times*, asked "What was your first big break?"

"When John Giorno pushed me down the stairs!" said Andy.

IN AUGUST 1963, Andy started shooting *Sleep*. It was an easy shoot. I loved to sleep. I slept all the time, twelve hours a day every day. It was the only place that felt good: complete oblivion, resting in a warm dream world, taking refuge in the lower realms. Everything awake was horrible. I was so unhappy. I would take a long nap every afternoon at 3:30 P.M., see a few more people, another short nap before Andy and I met and went out. Every time Andy telephoned, morning, afternoon, or night, I would be asleep. Andy would say *"What are you doing?"* and I would say "Sleeping." Or, he would say *"What are you doing? Don't tell me, I know!"*

We would get back to my place around one or two in the morning. I'd have another drink and take off my clothes, as Andy set up the tripod and camera, and messed around with some flood lights. Two minutes after my head hit the pillow, I was asleep. When I woke up the next morning, Andy would be gone, the house lights still on, and the floor littered with scraps of film and empty yellow boxes.

Andy would shoot for about three hours, until 5 A.M. when the sun rose, all by himself. Andy was on speed, everything was crystal clear. The Bolex was an early model. The camera had to be reloaded every three minutes and he had to rewind it by hand every twenty seconds. When he had the film developed, he discovered there was a jerk every twenty seconds. Two weeks shooting down the drain. Then Buddy Wirtshafter told him there was a gadget that plugs into the camera and plugs into the wall, and the camera rewinds automatically. We started over again. The shoot lasted a month. We stopped when he had taken thousands of rolls of film. Andy would look at them on the hand-cranked movie viewer, and say *"Oh, they're so beautiful!"*

This was Andy's first movie, and he didn't know how

to edit it into a film. Month after month went by and Andy couldn't figure out what to do with the thousands of rolls. He hired beautiful young Sarah Dalton to log the footage. Sarah meticulously and methodically looked at each roll on the primitive 16mm hand-cranked viewer in the cluttered back room. She drew story boards, little boxes with drawings of what was on each frame: the sleeping position, close up or full body shot, any movement, and she tried to reconstruct the sequence in which they were shot. It was a hopeless Herculean effort. It took her months and Andy still couldn't figure out how to edit it into a film. Finally Andy said, "We should just use anything!" He actually had shot eight hours of film, but he ended up using certain footage repeated over and over again. I stayed as far away as possible from the movie.

When *Sleep* was released, Andy got an enormous amount of publicity, people loved it and people hated it, which was his intention; and he launched his film career.

ON THURSDAY, October 31, 1963, Halloween night, Andy and I were going to an opening at Dick Bellamy's gallery on 57th Street. I went over to pick him up. *"My mother wants to meet you,"* Andy said.

"Why?" I said in surprise.

"She's heard about you!"

"What!"

"She's heard you on the stairs coming in and out!"

"Did she hear us fooling around in the hall last night?" I said horrified.

"She just wants to meet you."

Andy took me downstairs. The kitchen was in the back, a half floor below ground level. He knocked on the door and his mother opened it. *"Ma, this is John,"* said Andy.

His mother was an old Czech woman with a wide waist, gray hair, and a really sweet smile. She was wearing a floral cotton housedress. "Pleased to meet you," I said. We stood there looking in each other's eyes. She radiated a great kindness. This was a really important moment, Andy introducing me to his mother, whom nobody had met. It seemed like we really were lovers.

Andy and his mother talked about something in Czech. I managed to stick my head in her room. There was big brand-new Frigidaire, next to it on a table was a big new Motorola television, a kitchen table covered with floral oil cloth, a kitchen chair where she watched TV, a single bed against the far wall where she slept, and small religious statues on a dresser. It looked like the home of a Central European refugee. My eyes were out on stalks and I couldn't believe it was happening. Andy said she was very religious and went to church every day. He said he sometimes went with her on Sunday to St. Stephen's Church on Second Avenue and 15th Street, where there is a Czechoslovakian congregation.

"You're a good boy!" she said looking at me and smiling. Andy Warhol's mother approved of me. I was ecstatic.

Andy and I went laughing up the dark stairs. *"She likes you!"* said Andy happily.

I was very pleased with my accomplishment. And what a great Halloween, I thought, but I didn't say anything, because I didn't want to possibly hurt Andy.

We went to Dick Bellamy's gallery, where Dick had just broken up with his wife, Shindy, and Dick was in love with Sally Gross. The show was Bob Morris and his minimal cube boxes, another revolutionary moment in the history of sculpture.

ON DECEMBER 4th, 1963, Wynn Chamberlain gave me a birthday party at 222 Bowery. Wynn lived on the top or fifth floor. I would move into the third floor loft in 1966 when I returned from Morocco. William Burroughs would move into the mezzanine loft or Bunker in 1975. Now, in 1993, I live in, work in, and own both lofts.

It was flattering that Wynn wanted to give me a party. He called it a birthday party for a young poet named John Giorno, but it was just an excuse for Wynn to give another fabulous party. Everyone was there, the entire scene, all the Pop Artists, Patty and Claes Oldenburg, Jim Rosenquist, Roy Lichtenstein, etc., Bob Morris and Yvonne Rainer, Henry Geldzahler, and Frank O'Hara arrived with his retinue. About one hundred people. There was eighteen-year-old David Dalton and his seventeen-year-old sister Sarah Dalton, looking like sixteen-year-old beautiful twins. This was before Sally Stokes Cram married Wynn Chamberlain. Sally came with Prince Alexander Romanoff and Mimi Niscemi, and a contingent from the upper East Side. Kenneth Lane, a young kid from Detroit, who had just arrived in New York, appeared on the scene for the first time, and was about to make it big.

For live entertainment Wynn hired Tiny Tim to sing. It was before Tiny Tim became famous. Wynn had been to the Village Gate the week before, heard Tiny Tim, and thought he was totally great. After much haggling about the fee, Wynn paid him $150. He performed in the studio part of the loft, playing his plastic toy guitar. Tiny Tim was singing for about fifteen minutes, and was in the middle of *Tiptoe Through the Tulips*. The filmmaker Ron Rice, drunk and stoned on speed, hated Tiny Tim. He took off all his clothes, a straight man with a beautiful body, and started prancing around naked behind Tiny Tim. Ron tripped and fell back into the paper scrim which came crashing down, ending the performance, and Tiny Tim stalked out in a rage. This was a year before Ron Rice died in Mexico of tuberculosis and pneumonia.

It was a fabulous party. Andy Warhol and I were sitting on a couch in the living room near the front windows with old Ruth Yorck, or Countess Yorck as she liked to be called. She said imperiously, "Why are we here tonight?"

"It's John's birthday," said Andy.

She ignored him, and said again, "Why are we here tonight?"

"Today is my birthday and Wynn has given this party."

"Has he now! Aren't you a lucky boy!" Countess Yorck was a friend for forty years of an old friend of my mother's. She was always unkind to me, if not mali-

cious, even though she thought she was just mischie-
vous.

"It's so wonderful!" I wasn't going to let her spoil
anything.

"John is the star of my new movie," said Andy.

"You are a lucky boy!" she said, ending the conver-
sation. She didn't like Andy either.

Wynn called me into the studio for a champagne
toast and to cut the birthday cake and everyone sang
happy birthday.

Jonas Mekas was there. Naomi Levine arranged for
Andy to give the first screening of *Sleep* for Jonas the
following week in Wynn's loft. Jonas Mekas, with his
extravagant Romanian enthusiasm, loved *Sleep*, hailed
it as a work of genius, put a still-photo on the cover of
the next issue of *Film Culture*, and through the Film-
Makers Co-Op arranged for the world premiere of
Sleep in an old run-down movie theater near City Hall.
The first screening for Jonas Mekas, on an old clack-
ing projector on Wynn's studio wall at 222 Bowery,
launched Andy's underground film career.

IN NOVEMBER 1963, Andy and I went to Lita
Hornick's annual party in her Park Avenue apartment.
That year Lita gave it for the opening of LeRoi Jones's
plays *The Toilet* and *The Slave*. There was an enormous
number of people, Pinkerton guards, and that sweet
feeling when the rich slip into chaos.

Everyone knew that Andy wore a wig, but nobody
knew for sure. I wouldn't touch it. Several people
whispered to me that poet Willard Maas was going to

pull Andy's wig off. I couldn't believe he would do it. Andy was standing in front of a large black Ad Reinhardt painting, when sure enough Willard walked right up to Andy, grabbed hold of Andy's hair at the top of his head, and froze for a minute. Shrill silence. Then Willard let go and took his hand away. Apparently finding out it was a wig was enough for him, and he saved Andy the embarassment. Andy left the party immediately.

ONE MORNING in the beginning of January 1964, we talked about plans for the night on the phone. Andy was having his hair cut, there was an opening and a party. I was crashing, and had this disastrous hangover. I didn't get out of bed that day, and didn't go to the party. All I could do was lay my aching head on the pillow. That night after the party, at 11:30 P.M., Andy came to visit. He sat on my bed and we gossiped. "I had my hair cut by Mr. Kenneth today," said Andy. "He's so chic! He's so *fabulous!*" Mr. Kenneth was hair dresser to Jackie Kennedy. Andy went on endlessly, pleased about the event of his haircut. He started feeling me up through the covers.

"What did he do?" I said nervously.

"You're in a room all by yourself. They put a gown on you and you lie there," said Andy, as he slipped his hand under the covers, and started playing with my dick.

"You took off your clothes?" I said, resisting a little. I saw the inevitable coming.

"Oh no! Kenny is so *fabulous!*"

Generally speaking in those years Andy didn't have

sex with anyone. He had had enough of rejection, and just about closed down completely. Those sexual moments I had with Andy were unusual. I knew somehow they were important. 1963 was before Andy Warhol became famous. I did it because he wanted it so much. He was pathetic and I loved him.

I had this horrible hangover. Andy started sucking my cock. He was really good at it. He had a soft succulent mouth, quivering fingers, and a deep throat. I gave him a feel, and played with his hard cock and ass through the black Levi's and white jockey shorts, but that is not what he was interested in. He took my hand away. I left Andy's cock alone.

I lay there propped up on cushions, watching the silver hair going down on me. I knew he wore a wig, but I never touched it and never talked about it. Around the back of his neck, where the silver hair piece rose up from his real hair, there were five little quarter-inch bands of dyed color. First there was a thin band of blond, then a thin band of grey, then a thin band of brown, then a thin band of silver, and then a thin band of black nearest the skin, on top of which sat the wig. *"Will you please explain your hair!"* I said, as Andy sucked my cock. "There are five or more colors in your real hair . . . Look at that! Blond, what is blond doing there! And brown, and gray, and silver, and black. The colors are in a funny order! . . . *Would you please explain your hair, young man!* . . . Why did Kenny do that!" Andy was deep-throating me. "It is a hard-edge painting. You hair is a Frank Stella. Your hair is a work of art!"

"Oh, John!" said Andy, as he knelt on the floor with his elbows on the low bed. He kept on sucking, running his tongue around the head, licking the shaft of my dick, licking it like it was a lollypop. He was drooling saliva.

"I love your hair!" I gave him a load and he went home.

ANDY MADE A movie with me called *Hand Job*. It was the sequel to *Sleep*. He filmed a tight head shot of my face, while I was jerking off and cumming. It never got released, but it gave rise to Andy's next movie called *Blow Job*, which was the face of a guy getting a blow job. *Hand Job* fits historically in the sequence of head shot movies, after *Kiss*, and before *Haircut* and *Blow Job*.

Hand Job was shot in late January 1964, a month after Andy moved into the 47th Street Factory. Billy Linich, also called Billy Name, had just started making the Factory silver by putting aluminum foil on the walls. The factory was still this dismal industrial space. Billy first did the rusting corroded windows. He painted them silver, but the paint wasn't silver enough, then he tried foil from cigarette packs, and then he found Reynolds aluminum wrap. It was before Billy discovered silver mylar. Andy had only just cautiously decided aluminum foil was a good idea. *"Oh, it's so beautiful! Why not!"*

The set for *Hand Job* was the doorway of the sleazy toilet with the peeling-paint walls, and graffiti on the door. "Andy, this looks gorgeous!" I said. "It looks like a subway toilet!" It was a freezing-cold Saturday afternoon. There was no heat on weekends at the 47th Street Factory. Andy always shot his movies on weekends. Andy set up the camera and some lights. I smoked a joint and we were ready to shoot. I took out my dick, and said "Andy, suck it and get it hard." He got down on the dirty concrete floor and sucked. Andy slobbered around my dick to get it hard, so I could jerk off, and he could make a movie of my face while I was cumming. My cock was big and rock hard. I had my hand around the back of his neck and I deep-throat fucked his face. "When are we going to make this movie?" I said pulling him off.

Andy focused the camera on my face and I jerked off. I had to conjure up the most pornographic scenes from my promiscuous sex life, to keep it hard. It was so frigid cold in the Factory, I could see my breath.

Between rolls and changing film, Andy would come over and suck. His hands were shaking, only partly from the cold. It seemed like an important moment: Andy trembling and fragile, and this totally great idea. "This is hot! I can see my breath!" I took a hit of amyl nitrate and that really sent me off. After a long time, I came big globs of cum on the concrete floor. We finished about 5 o'clock on a dark depressing winter afternoon.

Andy never released *Hand Job*. In February 1964, he made a movie called *Blow Job*. Someone brought to the Factory this young, anonymous actor who was playing Shakespeare in the Park, a beautiful innocent guy who nobody knew and nobody saw again. Andy made *Blow Job* with him, the face of a man getting a blow job and cumming. Somebody sucked the guy's cock to get him ready and Willard Maas, who was sixty years old, sucked the guy off. I thought it was a great idea, as the concept was great anonymous sex, or how great anonymous sex is.

ANDY AND I were walking down St. Marks Place on October 27th, 1964 at about 5 P.M. We ran into a young art critic, Gene Swenson, in front of the St. Marks Baths, who said "Freddie Herko committed suicide." Freddie was dead. We stood there dumbstruck.

Freddie Herko was the star of Andy's movie *Haircut*. He was a beautiful brilliant young dancer. Earlier that afternoon, high on LSD and rehearsing a new dance in a sixth floor loft on Cornelia Street, with Mozart's Coronation Mass at full volume on the phonograph, he danced naked, jumping in a great leap out the window. It was sad for a moment, but then a wonderful warm feeling arose thinking about him. Freddie Herko had attained the absolute state of Nijinsky, and had also achieved the madness, like Nijinsky, plunging from a window to his death. A great accomplishment!

Andy's first words were *"Why didn't he tell me! . . . I would have made a movie! . . . I can't believe he did it and didn't tell me! . . . He knew I wanted to make another movie!"*

"Suicide!" I said. Another great idea! *Suicide*, the sequel to *Haircut*. I could have cried, but it was too glorious and joyful. *Suicide*. That was my movie.

"If you ever do it," said Andy, *"you better tell me!"*

Gene Swenson was wearing Levi's and I kept looking at his crotch and dick in the blue folds. Freddie was dead. (Gene would die in a car crash in 1969).

One of the first *Found Poems* I wrote from Freddie's obituary in the *Village Voice*:

Readings, dances
and music
will be given
tonight
(Thursday)
at Judson
Memorial Church
in memory of
Fred Herko,
the dancer
and choreographer
who last week
jumped to his death
from a sixth floor window
on Cornelia Street.
Herko
was a member
from the Judson Dance Theatre.

[From *The American Book of the Dead.*]

THE END OF 1964 was the end of my relations with Andy Warhol. We would soon be distant friends, occasionally meeting at parties. Andy went on to bigger and better things. At the time it seemed like I was being exploited, sucked in, chewed up, and spit out. Everyone always accused Andy Warhol of exploiting people, but the name of the game was exploitation. Andy exploited us and we exploited him. It always works both ways. We exploited Andy to become famous, which seemed the only real proof of being loved, but it was the 1960s and we were young and we didn't realize the other real proof was money. Andy understood both. All the rock 'n' roll cultural Superstars of the 1960s took all they could and then got rid of you.

The new Factory on 47th Street was taking shape and I was excluded. Jerry Malanga, an undergraduate at Wagner College on Staten Island, worked for Andy, sweeping floors and running errands. When Jerry came to power at the Factory, I was suddenly excluded.

As in all relationships that are breaking up, it was very painful for me, because I loved Andy. The more Andy got rid of me, the more I wanted to be his friend, his lover, anything. Andy got rid of me the way he got rid of all the Factory Superstars, one by one, after he finished using them. Unlike the other Superstars, many of whom were destroyed, when he got rid of me, I went on to bigger and better things, too. In December 1964, I met William Burroughs and Brion Gysin. William and I began a friendship that is still deep and loving thirty years later. In 1966 and '67, Bob Rauschenberg and I were lovers; in 1968 and '69, Jasper Johns and I were lovers; but those are other stories. I soon completely forgot about Andy Warhol.

IN 1967, PETER Schjeldahl and Mother Press published a book of my selected poems. Peter suggested I ask Andy Warhol to do the book cover, as Peter thought my poems were Pop poems. I asked Andy, and after several months, he came up with the idea that the front cover should be a scumbag laminated between clear plastic, with *Poems by John Giorno* stenciled on it. Each book with its own scumbag. We agreed they must be used scumbags. I loved the idea.

However, I explained that Mother Press printed one thousand copies, plus a signed limited edition of one hundred. "Where are we going to get all those scum bags?" I said. "I don't have time to fill them all, although I'd like to."

"Oh, we can pick them up on the street," said Andy. I thought this was a great idea. But it was also a bit difficult logistically. I was relieved, as it was Peter's idea to say no, and I was finished with Andy.

In those years, Bob Rauschenberg and I were lovers; and Peter suggested and it seemed only natural for me to ask Bob to do the cover. Bob, with great love, made a fabulously beautiful work of art for the book cover.

ANDY STARTED MAKING the Death paintings in September 1963. Suicides, car crashes, atomic bombs, race riots, and electric chairs. Many of them were from the photographs that Wynn Chamberlain's cop boyfriend Jimmy O'Neill had given to Andy in the summer of 1963. The disaster photos came with the Ten Most Wanted Men.

In November 1961, my really good friend Marcia Stillman committed suicide. She had taken some LSD before Thanksgiving dinner. Her straight family lived at 530 Park Avenue at 61st Street. She was eighteen years old and very beautiful. She felt a little dizzy and hot, so she got up from the table and went to her bedroom. It was a very warm Thanksgiving afternoon. She sat on the window ledge to get a breath of air. She fell eight floors to her death on the cement courtyard between the apartment building and Christ Church. Marcia's death became an obsession.

I asked Andy to make a painting of Marcia's suicide. The plan was for Jimmy O'Neill to get the actual police photo of Marcia laying dead on the ground, from the police precinct where she lived. I was completely obsessed with it. I kept asking Wynn if Jimmy had gotten the photo yet. No progress was being made on a really good idea. One day Andy said, "I found it in the photos Jimmy gave me."

Andy had found the photo of a girl who had committed suicide by jumping out of a window at Bellevue Hospital, and was laying face down on a cobblestone street, surrounded by three policemen and a male nurse leaning over her dead body. Andy made the Suicide painting, silkscreening the image twelve times, black on a white canvas, seven feet square.

One night in early November 1963 was the exhilarating moment when I arrived at Andy's house and the canvas was stapled up on the wall. Marcia's suicide! Absolute joy and bliss and clarity, I felt, standing there looking at it. And it turned out to be one of the great paintings of the 20th century. Andy was radiant, and said, *"Oh, I know, it's so great!"*

It took me a few months to pry it out of Andy. I kept saying "You said you wanted to give me something. I want Marcia's Suicide."

Andy kept saying *"I made it for you."* Finally one day he said "How are we going to get it to your place?" I carried very carefully the large roll of canvas to East 74th Street. Andy came one morning a few weeks later and stretched it. *"You don't know what I've given you!"*

"I do! I do! I do!" I said hugging him.

The painting hung there gloriously until January 1965, when I quit being a Wall Street stockbroker, gave up my carriage house on East 74th Street, and moved into Ted Berrigan's old apartment on East 9th Street between Avenues B and C. I had the *Suicide* painting moved there. I had it un-stretched and re-stretched. In January 1966, I gave up that apartment, when I went to Tangier for six months to visit Brion Gysin. I had the canvas rolled and moved to my mother's house on Long Island, where I've stored my archive for all these years.

In 1970, Les Levine, who was doing a little buying and selling of art for profit, said "I know somebody who wants to buy your Andy Warhol. He says he'll pay $30,000 cash." I hadn't thought about the painting in years. My obsession with Andy, Marcia's suicide and Andy's painting had been liberated, dissolved and forgotten. A collector named Peter Brant wanted to buy it. I was a poet, poor and paying bills with a small amount of money. I didn't want to sell it, but what the fuck,

$30,000 out of the blue. It seemed like a great idea. I sold it to him. The last blessing of the 1960s. One sweet moment of reward. $30,000 spent playfully was a lot of money in 1970. I had infinite love and thankfulness for Andy, who I rarely saw. Now I was in the William Burroughs/Brion Gysin configuration, and they hated Andy's work, and didn't think very much of him. The worlds were parallel, very occasionally overlapping.

In the fall of 1970, the Factory Superstars, many of whom had been abandoned and felt exploited, were giving Andy a hard time about money and why they were never paid anything. Andy went around saying *"John Giorno is my highest paid Superstar. He got $30,000."* Then Andy tried to get some of the money. He sent me a message, why didn't I have him paint my portrait for $15,000. I said no!

In 1987, around the time of the Sotheby auctions, one of Andy's *Disaster* paintings sold privately in Europe for one million dollars. About that time, the Stedelijk Museum in Amsterdam bought the *Suicide* painting. Art historians are unanimous that *Suicide*, now called *Bellevue*, is the best of the *Disaster* paintings, and is now worth three million dollars. No regrets, as the $30,000 bought me a million dollars of generosity and joy.

ANDY WARHOL WAS in Milan the last week of January 1987, for the opening of his last show, *The Last Supper* paintings. From Milan he went to Geneva and Zurich, where there were endless parties given by Thomas Amann and other rich and famous people. At all the various dinners and lunches, Andy kept meeting an Italian woman, who was short and heavy with long black hair. Andy thought she wanted to kill him. Andy kept saying *"Oh, she's trying to kill me!"*

Then Andy freaked out and left for New York two days early. He was supposed to stay a week in Zurich, but the woman really upset him, and he left after five days. It had been arranged that when he returned he would have the kidney stone laser operation. When he arrived, there happened to be an empty hospital bed. Andy went into the hospital, and was dead two days later.

It is possible that Andy Warhol misread the information the woman was giving him. She was not trying to kill him. She was telling him he was soon going to die. Whether she was clairvoyant and telling what was going to happen, or whether she was a projection of Andy's own intuition, she was trying to tell him something important. Andy's mistake was he didn't listen or understand she was telling him to prepare for death.

Andy died very unexpectedly, and was very attached to life. He was totally grasping to everything, as witnessed by the magnitude of his fame and wealth. Now that he's dead, he's lost everything. It is possible that Andy refused to believe he was dead, refused to go on, may have not let go, clinging to this world from the afterworld, and stayed for a while as a ghost, lingering for some time in this world as a spirit. The moment of death is very important. When you die unexpectedly, fear can arise, and from fear sometimes anger arises, sending you to the hell worlds and back again.

As much as he probably loved the sale of his estate at Sotheby's, because it made him so rich and gave him such enormous publicity, it undoubtedly also caused him great suffering. He would have seen them auction off everything one by one. (The dead can see and hear for some time, only having lost their bodies, they see and hear through habit, the way you do when you sleep and dream.) Andy could see the objects he had so obsessively collected being lost. As Fran Lebowitz said at the Sotheby's auction, "Andy must be furious he's dead!"

When Andy was asked what he would like his next reincarnation to be, he said *"A great big diamond on the finger of Elizabeth Taylor!"* You can't be reincarnated as an inanimate object, but you can be reborn as a spirit who dwells in such an object.

NOW IN 1989, writing these words, drunk and stoned in the Bunker at 222 Bowery, I summon Andy to come and tell me what to write. I clap my hands three times and call him from the dead. I call Andy from the dead, he comes, and his consciousness is next to me in the chair or resting in my heart. I say, "Andy, tell me what I should say and tell me how I should say it. I want to make it fantastic for you!" The dead who have hung around have nothing else to do. It's a pleasure writing about the dead. It's all they've got.

Being a Tibetan Buddhist, I have been sad to think that Andy may be trapped in the Bardo. I often in my meditation send him energy and blessings, radiating light from my heart to his consciousness, in hope that it may help release him. Sometimes in the beginning I got the feeling that Andy didn't want me to do this, that he wanted to stay wherever he was, grasping onto Andy Warhol; or it made him nervous, as it did when he was alive; or he still doesn't understand and is just laughing, *"Oh John!"*; but now when I do, I get a much better feeling.

One of the concepts of my memoirs is: what somebody does in bed, intimate facts about their sexual preference, details about what they like to do and how they love, are great clues to understanding their work, are absolutely necessary to know their work completely, and viewed with compassion can help illuminate the wisdom of their work.

Everyone in the world would prefer you to know the good things and not the bad. Andy tried to hide everything that was real about himself. If Andy were alive, he would hate the things I've written about him, but he's dead, it's all he's got, and I feel he loves it. It gives him more publicity, more myth, more everything Andy Warhol. Andy has lost everything, except these stories and his art.

I LEARNED THAT Andy Warhol had died on a CBS TV news brief on Sunday morning at 7:40, on February 22nd, 1987. I had been up all night working at 222 Bowery. I felt numb, more than anything else. I kept checking my thoughts to see if I felt sad. I didn't feel anything. Very Andy Warhol, I thought. I realized later that in dying Andy came alive for me again.

I saw Andy more the last year of his life than I had for fifteen years. Maybe it was because I went to lots of parties that year. The last great parties before everyone died of AIDS. At the Palladium parties, when it opened in May 1986, Andy was really kind to me and we had these endearing exchanges. Andy Warhol was dead. I went to sleep on a cold, empty, depressing winter morning.

At 2:30 P.M., I called William Burroughs and told him the news. William was very concerned. Those moments finding out that someone has died are shocking, and offer a feeling of great clarity. At 4:30 P.M., Victor Bockris called me with the news. Victor had been working for two years on Andy's biography. Victor was very shaken. After we hung up, I cried briefly, for about ten seconds. Victor's loss made the loss real. Andy's body was whisked off immediately by his family for a funeral in Pittsburgh. Immediately after someone powerful dies is very powerful; you can feel it and taste it.

A GREAT MEMORIAL service for more than two thousand invited guests was held at St. Patrick's Cathedral on April 1, 1987. The atmosphere was electrifying. I sat between Victor Bockris and Billy Name. I hadn't seen Billy in twenty years, and from a pencil-thin unbelievably beautiful boy, he'd become fat and bald with a long beard. There was a high Mass and a huge number of people received Holy Communion, among them: Viva in a broad-brim black hat, Don Johnson, Liza

Minnelli on the arm of Halston, and Claus von Bulow. Some people observed it was a triumph of the Catholics. It was a heavenly display of worldly power.

Afterwards, Fred Hughes, Brigid Berlin and the Factory gave a fabulous lunch for 250 people at a club that Steve Rubell had just bought on West 46th Street that formerly was Billy Rose's Diamond Horseshoe Nightclub. Everyone was there who had survived from the 1960s, from Lou Reed (who appeared deeply moved) to Debbie Harry. I got a champagne high, and it felt great being there because I knew everyone, and I strongly sensed the presence of Andy's consciousness there. It was the beginning of Andy Warhol's triumph in death.

ON FEBRUARY 1, 1989, I went to the gala opening of the Andy Warhol Retrospective at the Museum of Modern Art, curated by Kynaston McShine. There were all of Andy's great works. Andy was dead, and Andy was there. I went to the cocktail reception and private viewing that began at 7 P.M., followed by the David Rockefeller black-tie dinner for five hundred, and the opening party for three thousand people. Lita Hornick, wearing a couture gown of green brocade by Scaasi and a huge diamond necklace, looked like a dowager empress. I wore black tie.

We arrived at 7:15 P.M., almost nobody had come yet, and the galleries were empty. It was somewhat overwhelming, seeing the show fresh in its first moments. Room after room of paintings I hadn't seen or thought about for twenty-five years. I remembered when they were painted and could recall the strong feelings associated with first seeing them in Andy's house or at the first show in 1962. There were only one or two people in each gallery and I knew almost everyone. Robert Mapplethorpe was in a wheel chair, two months before he died of AIDS. The sparseness and selectness was very Andy: money and power.

I was standing in front of the Troy Donahue painting, which I hadn't seen since 1962. Just remembering the name Troy Donahue was perplexing. I turned and there was Henry Geldzahler. We kissed and I said, "What do you think!"

Henry said "I'm sad."

"Why?"

"Because Andy isn't here," said Henry. I was about to say, do you really think Andy isn't here, but we laughed instead.

I continued walking through the galleries—each painting looked slightly more bewildering in absolute clarity—shaking hands with people, and saying, "Hello!"

I was standing in front of the small *Marilyn Monroe* paintings, which I hadn't seen in twenty-five years. I turned and there was Henry Geldzahler standing next to me again. "I can't believe it! I once owned that!" said Henry, pointing to the *Turquoise Marilyn* and letting out a long sigh. "I can't believe I sold it!" Andy had given it to Henry in 1962, and Henry had sold it in the early 1970s.

Fifteen minutes later I was standing in front of the

Suicide painting that Andy had given me in 1963 and which I had sold in 1970 for $30,000. The painting was now called *Bellevue II*, and was there on loan from the Stedelijk Museum in Amsterdam, which had bought it for one million dollars. I remembered Henry's words "I can't believe it! I once owned that! I can't believe I sold it!" There *Suicide* was in all its profoundly depressing magnificence.

Entering the next gallery, I was surprised seeing the large freestanding plexiglass silk-screen painting of *Sleep*, and had a rush of exhilaration. Andy had made it in 1965, after I stopped seeing him, and I had only seen it once in a gallery. I remembered asking Andy in 1963, when he wanted to give me a present, "Make me like Marilyn Monroe!" Indeed he had! There was a painting of me sleeping hanging with paintings of Marilyn Monroe. Andy Warhol was completely empty and completely fulfilling.

In the next gallery was Andy's *Gold Marilyn Monroe*, the small color face on a big gold canvas. It had been in the entrance of Andy's first show at the Stable Gallery in 1962, where it gave me goose-bumps looking at it. This painting should be revered, as is the *Mona Lisa* in the Louvre. Philip Johnson bought it, and had given it to MOMA in 1964. The gold paint had faded into a black lustre of inexplicable power. I was looking at the sacred relic of a dead king.

Then I went to the bar and had a drink. Fran Lebowitz was sitting at a cocktail table, all by herself, drinking a glass of Perrier, and being very serious so she could be very funny. I told her I was writing about Andy and that I wanted to use her words from the Sotheby's auction: "Andy must be so furious he's dead!" Fran said very seriously, "Go ahead and use it!"

The David Rockefeller dinner was boring and pleasant. Nobody is invited to those dinners other than very rich old people and very famous old people. I was shocked to see Keith Haring sitting opposite me at the round dinner table. "I'm so happy you're here!" said Keith, who looked great, and said he was going on a vacation, the first time ever, to Spain and Morocco. That night I didn't know that Keith Haring had just that day found out he had AIDS and Kaposi sarcoma. Keith and I always ran into each other at the strangest times, funny karma we had, of all the people I end up sitting with Keith at Andy Warhol's last supper.

Donald Marron, President of MOMA, gave a little talk thanking Knoll International and the Drue Heinz Foundation for sponsoring the show. He didn't mention that none of the usual corporate sponsors wanted to touch the show because Andy was gay and used drugs, even though Andy hadn't used drugs for over twenty years. The retrospective was in jeopardy up to a month and a half before it opened, when Drue Heinz gave an additional very large gift.

I was the only one of the old Superstars invited to the dinner. Afterwards we grandly went downstairs to the party opening the show, where three thousand people were jammed together in a screaming writhing hell world. Descending gods, just like when Andy and

I fell down the stairs. At the bottom was: Ultra Violet, Gerard Malanga, David Bourdon, and a zoo of people pushing in every direction. I left almost immediately. There was the Andy Warhol impersonator, the guy who looks identical to Andy, wears the same Andy wig, and speaks in the same voice. A perfect fake Andy Warhol. He came up to me, and said, *"Oh hello, John!"* I got goose bumps. His voice was the same sound, pitch and resonance that would have come from Andy. For me, he was a live voodoo doll occupied by Andy for the night. Andy was everywhere that night. The dead can see what you see, hear what you say, know what you think, and feel what you feel, if they're interested enough. It's called the suffering of the dead.

I'm sure Andy was interested.

OVER THE LAST twenty-five years, Andy Warhol was asked many times, *"What are you afraid of? Are you afraid of anything?"* Andy would always say in his inimitable fashion, as documented in many interviews, *"I'm afraid to die in my sleep!"* Andy died unexpectedly in his sleep. When you're dead, you're all by yourself.

In September 1987, I went to the Whitney Museum with Victor Bockris, and saw a forty-minute excerpt from *Sleep*. It was embarrassing, like looking at baby pictures of before you lost your baby fat. I was a big baby and a big piece of meat.

I love to sleep to this day. I want to stay asleep for as long as I can. I go down deep and stay there. Down deep into the underworld relishing the opiates of delusion. Of my many luxuries, sleep is the luxury I

love best. The most rewarding! The ignorance of the
god worlds, resting in the lower realms. Sleep is
wonderful, the best thing about living. Everyone is
asleep.

1989

SUICIDE SUTRA

EVERYONE IS INVITED to participate in this poem. This is an audience participation poem. Please follow the instructions as you read them, and tighten the muscles of your body. Tighten each individual muscle and hold it. You should become uptight.

You can't
remember
where you
are,
you have forgotten
who you are,
you can't even

remember
what the words
mean,
and you want
to change it
and you want to
change it
and you want to change it
and you want to change it,
and you don't
know how
to do it.

Tighten
your fingers,
tighten
your hands,
tighten
your wrists,
tighten
your forearms
and your elbows,
tighten
your upper arms
and tighten
your shoulders.

You are
in jail
you are in jail
you are in jail,

you are locked
in this space,
it is dark
and smelly,
and filthy,
completely
depressing
completely depressing.

You are
alone
you are alone,
and you are
lonely

and you are lonely
and you are lonely,
and it's eating
your heart
out,
and there's
no way
out.

Tighten
your shoulders,
tighten
your back muscles,
tighten
the curve
in your back,
and tighten

the cheeks
of your ass.

The air
is liquid
the air is liquid,
thick
and heavy
pressing
in
on you.

Giant
boulders
are crushing
against
each other,
giant boulders
are crushing you,
and they are crushing you,
and they are
killing you
and they are killing you.
The air
around
your body
turns
to solid
rock,
and it's smothering
you

and it's smothering you
and it's smothering you,
and you can feel it
inside your chest
breaking
your heart.

Tighten
your chest
muscles,
tighten
your stomach
muscles,
tighten
your gut,
tighten the cheeks
of your ass,
your rib
cage
is locked.

You are
angry
you are angry
you are angry,
and you really
hate it
and you really hate it
and you really hate it,
and you want
to scream

and you want to scream,
but you can't
but you can't
because
the sound
is locked
in your throat
the sound is
locked in your throat.

They are pulling
your arms
off
they are pulling your arms off,
they are ripping
your arms off
your body,
they are twisting
your head
off
they are twisting your head off.

Tighten
your neck,
tighten
your forehead,
tighten
your nose,
tighten
your lips,
tighten

your cheeks,
tighten
your jaw,
tighten
the skin
on your skull.

Your eyes
are open
your eyes are open,
and your eyes
are popping
out
of your head
and your eyes are popping
out of your head.

You are in a doorless
burning
house
you are in a doorless burning house,
enclosed
enclosed
enclosed inside
another
doorless
burning
house
inside another doorless burning house,
inside
another

inside another,
and you are crying
and you are crying
and you are crying.

Tighten
your shoulders,
tighten
your arms,
tighten
your wrists,
tighten
your hand,
tighten
your fingers.

There is
a gun
in your hand
there is a gun in your hand,
a 38-caliber
revolver,
and it's pointing
at your face
and it's pointing at your face
and it's pointing at your face,
and you pull
the trigger
and you pull
and you pull the trigger,
the bullet

shoots
slowly
the bullet shoots slowly
toward
your head
shoots slowly toward your head,
you are committing
suicide
you are committing suicide
you are committing suicide,
and it smashes
into your face
and it smashes into your face
and it smashes into your face,
and blows
your skull
open
and blows your skull open,
blood
and brains
and flesh
and skin
and hair
fly
into the air.

You are dying
you are dying
you are dying
you are dying,
and you're still

trying
to hold it
together,
trying
to hold
it in,
trying to hold
the bloody
mess
as it scatters
in the room.

Tighten
your shoulders,
straighten
your back,
suck in
your crotch
and your asshole,
tighten
your gut.

You are dead
you are dead
you are dead
you are dead,
and it's the same
and it's the same
and it's the same,
nothing
has changed

nothing
nothing
nothing has changed,
only it's a little
worse,
it's more
horrible
it's more horrible,
you're just
in another
hell,
and there's
no way
out
and there's no
way out
and there's no way out.

There's nothing
else
to do,
but tighten
your thigh
muscles,
and tighten
your knees,
tighten
your calves,
tighten
your ankles,
tighten

your feet,
and tighten
your toes.

There is
no time
off,
and if you go
to sleep
you blow it,
you are totally
lost
you are totally lost
and you have forgotten
you are dead
and you have forgotten you are dead.

Go over
your body
and tighten
the muscles
that have loosened,
every muscle
must be totally
intensified,
you are hard
as a rock.

You hear
the long
low

roar
of a jet
plane
you hear the long low roar
of a jet plane,
and it gets
louder
and louder
and it gets louder
and louder
and it gets louder and louder
into a piercing
shriek
overhead.

A napalm
bomb
explodes
napalm
napalm
napalm
sliding
everywhere
sliding everywhere,
and you are covered
with burning
napalm
and you are covered
with burning napalm,
for an instant

you can't believe
it's really happening.

Your skin
is burning
your skin is burning
your skin is burning,
every inch of you
is burning,
napalm
that sticks
and can't be
rubbed off
or put out,
and has to burn out.

Your skin
is blistering
your skin is blistering,
and there are blisters
inside
those blisters
and there are blisters
inside those blisters,
and cracking blisters
inside those,
and more
inside those
and more inside those.

Your muscles
are cooking,
you smell
like a juicy
steak
barbecuing
on a charcoal
grill.

Your eyes
are open
and your eyes
are popping out
of your head,
and your eyes
are burning
and your eyes are
burning
and your eyes are burning,
and you have to get
out of here.

You lean
forward
on your left
leg,
lean gently
forward,
and suck in
your asshole,

and suck in
your crotch,
and straighten
your back.

Feel
the energy
inside
your gut
running
up
your spine,
flowing
in a white
channel
up into
your head,
and you go
slowly
and you go slowly
up
and up
and up
and up,
it's like you're
a baby
being born
from your mother,
it's like being
squeezed
through

a steel net,
and you go
higher
and you go higher,
and higher
and higher
and higher.

It's like being
born,
a flower
opening,
and it is effortless
and it is effortless
and it is effortless,
and becomes
cooler
and cooler
and cooler,
and calm
and calm
and calm.

You haven't gotten
anywhere,
only
here.

1973

GIORNO
POETRY SYSTEMS

A HUNDRED YEARS ago when you had nothing to do and you were home alone, going crazy, bored and anxious and lonely, or just plain tired, or with a simple longing for absolute wisdom, what you did was read. You sat in a chair or curled up on a bed, lit by a candle, and read a novel or a book of poems. That's why those literary forms flourished for all those centuries: there was a need. You can only take people where they want to go.

Nowadays, when I'm home alone, de-pressed and irritated, just trying to deal

with my mind, or feeling good and want-
ing to be entertained, one of the last things
I think of doing is reading a book. I watch
television, listen to a CD or cassette, look at
a video, play the radio, talk on the phone,
or go to a performance.

In 1965, I stumbled onto the concept that a poet can connect with an audience using all the entertainments of ordinary life: watching television, listening to albums, using the telephone, etc. This gave rise to Giorno Poetry Systems: creating Dial-A-Poem in 1968; producing 28 LPs, CDs, and cassettes; making poetry videos, videopaks and films; elevating the poetry reading to a high art form; innovating the use of technology in poetry; using radio and television; organizing performances, benefits, and tours; the John Giorno Band; Consumer Product Poetry, publishing poetry on the surface of ordinary objects; and silkscreen and lithograph Poem Prints.

Compact Disc, LP, Cassette, Video

Cash Cow: The Best of Giorno Poetry Systems, 1965–1993: CD, 1993, GPS 044.
Paul Alberts, Shubert / Mozart CD, 1992, GPS 043.
Like A Girl, I Want You to Keep Coming LP, CD, cassette, 1989, GPS 040.
Smack My Crack LP, CD, cassette, 1987, GPS 038.
A Diamond Hidden in the Mouth of a Corpse LP, cassette, 1986, GPS 035.
Better an Old Demon Than a New God LP, 1984, GPS 033.
Lenny Kaye Connection LP, 1984, GPS 032.

You're a Hook, The 15 Year Anniversary of Dial-A-Poem LP, 1983, GPS 030.
One World Poetry LP, 1982, GPS 028-029.
Life Is a Killer LP, 1982, GPS 027.
Who You Staring At? Glenn Branca/John Giorno LP, 1982, GPS 025.
Polyphonix 1 LP, 1982, GPS 024.
You're the Guy I Want to Share My Money With: Laurie Anderson, William Burroughs, John Giorno 1981, LP GPS 020-021, cassette GPS 022-023, CD & cassette GPS 042.
Sugar, Alcohol, & Meat LP, 1980, GPS 018-019.
The Nova Convention 1979, LP GPS 014-15, cassettes GPS 016-017.
Big Ego LP, 1978, GPS 012-013.

John Giorno & Anne Waldman LP, 1977, GPS 010-011.
Totally Corrupt LP, 1976, GPS 008-009.
William S. Burroughs/John Giorno LP, 1976, GPS 006-007.
Biting off the Tongue of a Corpse LP, 1975, GPS 005.
Disconnected LP, 1974, GPS 003-004.
The Dial-A-Poem Poets LP, 1972, GPS 001-002.
Raspberry & Pornographic Poem LP, 1967.

Giorno Video Pak 4, Gang of Souls by Maria Beatty, 1990, GPS 039.
Giorno Video Pak 3, It's Clean, It Just Looks Dirty, 1987, GPS 037
Giorno Video Pak 2, Burroughs, The Movie by Howard Brookner, 1985, GPS 034.
Giorno Video Pak 1, 1984, GPS 031.

Books of Poetry

Du Musst Brennen Um Zu Strahlen, Stop Over Press, Berlin, 1992.
Grasping at Emptiness, Kulchur Foundation, New York, 1985.
Suicide Sutra, Christian Bourgois Editions (French translation), Paris, 1980.
Shit, Piss, Blood, Pus, & Brains, The Painted Bride Press, Philadelphia 1977.
Cancer in My Left Ball, Something Else Press, 1973.

Cum, Adventures In Poetry, New York, 1971.

Cunt, Marz Verlag (German translation), Dharmstadt, 1970.

Balling Buddha, Kulchur Press, New York, 1970.

Johnny Guitar, Angel Hair Books, New York, 1969.

Poems by John Giorno, Mother Press, New York, 1967.

The American Book of the Dead, 1964.

The **John Giorno Band** performed in New York at the Bottom Line, Ritz, Beacon, Palladium, and CBGBs, and toured extensively: Boston, Toronto, Montreal, Detroit, Kansas City, Oklahoma City, Fort Worth, Tallahassee, Atlanta, Miami, etc., 1984–88.

Radio

With the release of each album, 400 are sent free to FM and college radio stations across the country, where they are put in heavy rotation, and are played for decades. Millions of people hear the records, 1967–93.

Satellite Radio Poets, 1981; and **The Poetry Experiment, WBAI**, a weekly series of one-and-a-half hour programs, 1976–79.

WPAX, 1971, radio programs recorded in New York with Abbie Hoffman, and broadcast on Radio Hanoi to American soldiers fighting in South Vietnam.

Radio Free Poetry, 1969, The Software Show, The Jewish Museum, New York. Broadcast through the electrical wiring of the building onto an empty FM channel, where the signal radiated several hundred feet, and was picked up by museum visitors on transistor radios.

Poem Prints (*silkscreen and lithography*)

Durham Press, 1992–93.
George Mulder Fine Art, 1991.
Nova Scotia College of Art (Lithography Press), 1973.
Something Else Press, 1973.
Giorno Poetry Systems, 1968–93.

Movies

Poetry in Motion, directed by Ron Mann, 1982.
September on Jessore Road, starring Allen Ginsberg, directed by John Giorno, 1971.

Performances, Events, Benefits, & Tours (*short list*)

Where the Rubber Meets the Road, AIDS Treatment Project Benefit, Beacon, New York, 1987.
The Red Night Tour, 1981.
The Nova Convention, 1978
The Nyingmapa Buddhist Benefits, 1971–80.
The 1st Annual New Year's Benefit, St. Mark's

Church, New York, December 31, 1969 & January 1, 1970 (34 hour continuous).

The Release Benefits, St. Mark's Church, New York, 1969–70.

Central Park Poetry Events, New York, 1968.

Consumer Product Poetry, publishing poetry on the surface of ordinary objects: Matchbook Poems, T-Shirt Poems, Flag Poems, Chocolate Bar Poems, Window Curtain Poems, Cigarette Package Poems, and included in the design on commercial packaging, 1968–74.

Electronic Sensory Poetry Environments, ESPE, innovating the use of performance, technology, and music in poetry readings:
Subway Poem, 1965.
Chromosome & Raspberry, 1967.
Purple Heart, 1968.
Johnny Guitar, 1969.
Cum, 1970.

Dial-A-Poem

John Giorno created Dial-A-Poem in 1968, when millions of people called and listened to poetry. Dial-A-Poem was the first time the telephone was used to communicate to a large audience, beginning a new era in telecommunications, mass media, and Dial-A-something.

Dial-A-Poem, The Architectural League of New York, 1968.

Dial-A-Poem, The Museum of Contemporary Art, Chicago, 1969.

Dial-A-Poem, The Museum of Modern Art, New York, 1970.

Dial-A-Poem, The Philadelphia Museum of Art, 1972.

Operaesji Fers (Frisian language), Leeuwarden, The Netherlands, 1969; Dial-A-Poem (Dutch), Amsterdam, The Netherlands, 1970.

Dial-A-Poem, Cardiff, Wales, 1970; London, England, 1970.

Dial-A-Poem, Brussels, Belgium; Paris, France; Zurich and Basel, Switzerland.

Dial-A-Poem, Berlin and 12 cities in West Germany (Frankfurt, Hamburg, Bremen, Kiel, Nuremburg, Mannheim, Munich, Stuttgart, Dusseldorf, etc.), 1983.

DIAL-A-POEM, Albany, New York, 1973.

PHONE-A-POEM, Cambridge, Massachusetts, 1975.

DIAL-A-POEM, Indianapolis, Indiana, 1976.

TELEPOEM, Venice, California, 1976.

DIAL-A-POEM, Louisville, Kentucky, 1976; Amberson, Pennsylvania, 1980; Providence, Rhode Island, 1980; Montreal, Canada, 1985; etc.

And inspired: Dial-A-Joke, Dial-A-Horoscrope, Dial-A-Santa Claus, Dial-A-Recipe, Dial-A-Children's Story, Dial-A-Soap, Dial-Sports, Wall Street Stock

Quotations, Off Track Betting, Suicide Hotline, Lotto, Dial-Porn, Dial-Love, etc.

All this activity is the poet extending poetry to meet the audience. In this dynamic relationship, the poet is actively involved in investigating and expanding the connection, and intimately involved in every moment of the process, from the first idea through every stage of production to the last clapping hand. A hundred years ago when you wanted to communicate with someone you wrote something on a piece of paper and a man on a horse rode away with it. Now we want to go live to millions, faster than the speed of light, with no compromise, and I am living proof that anyone can do it. You just got to do it.

EPILOGUE

THE POEMS IN this book were conceived to be heard, in performance, and on a CD, cassette, and video.

While I am writing the poem, I perform it with a live microphone, and when it is completed, I rehearse it, trying to bring forth and develop the melodies inherent in the words and phrases. The poet talks directly to an audience, one to one, with perfect sound, heart contact and wisdom content. Writing a poem that is meant to be heard in performance is different than writing a poem meant to be read in a book. Sometimes when I have a problem with some words, I visualize an audience in front of me, perform the words to them, and the problem becomes apparent and gets solved. I want to jump inside your heart.

The words are empowered by the wind or breath flowing through the nerve channels of the body. First I take some deep breaths, then breathe air deep into the lungs, slowly pressing it down, letting the stomach muscles relax, letting it settle deeper and deeper into the bottom of the lungs, and holding it there for as long as I can, then slowly releasing it and doing it again. A pearl-shaped bag of air forms at the bottom of the belly, and pressing the air down and keeping it there causes heat to build. When it gets hot, I am ready to perform. Sweat and poetry. The heat from these centers, combined with the wisdom content of the words, is the power of the poem.

The written word is very important to all my work; without it there would be no poem. The words of a poem first arise in my mind as sound, second are written down long hand on paper, third are typed into the computer, and then are made into a performance, song or sound composition, and placed on a diskette, become a Poem Print and a book.

Spoken word, using breath and heat, pitch and volume, and the melodies inherent in the language, risking technology and music, and a deep connection with an audience, is the fulfillment of a poem. It's the entertainment industry (you got to sweeten the deal) transmitting an absolute awareness of ordinary mind. After a performance in CBGBs, someone said to me, "I hate poetry, but I love poets who sweat." After a performance in Columbus, Ohio, a woman said to me,

"I don't know much about poetry, but I love a poet who makes me feel something." For me performing poetry is sustained sexual activity in a golden age of promiscuity. You can never be too generous.

During a performance in Avignon, France in November 1991, a skinhead discharged rocket fireworks at me, whizzing around and barely missing my head and body. They landed on the audience behind the stage (nobody got hurt). "Une fusillade," as they say in French. Afterward, outside, he came up to me and said sadly, "I'm burning, but I'm not shining." I looked at him and thought, You're burning from all the beer you've drunk, and probably the speed you've taken. Sweat shines from the fire of wisdom arising in the heart, as a result of realizing the empty primordially pure nature of reality. But I didn't say anything, because he wouldn't have understood—*You got to burn to shine.*

SERPENT'S TAIL

HIGH RISK BOOKS